HOW TO ANALYZE PEOPLE

A COMPLETE GUIDE ON HOW TO USE BODY LANGUAGE AND IMPROVE YOUR SKILLS WITH PEOPLE THROUGH

MIND CONTROL AND DARK PSYCHOLOGY.

Table of Contents

Introduction

There is very little more disappointing than failure to thrive in your relationship with people. Whether it is with family, friends or your colleagues at work it, that failure. makes you feel like an outsider. It has a way of stripping you of your confidence and leaving you with a strong sense of disappointment. This used to be me and at some point in my life, I would sit in the corner and declare that I had no place in this world and for a while I was comfortable in this illusion I created for myself. I even deceived myself into believing that I was comfortable being the outsider. But you know the thing with illusions, at some point you have to confront the reality of things and the reality is that we need people in our lives.

Humans are created for interaction and relations. However, communication is what establishes those relationships. Not bond, not obligation not even filial affiliations; just good old fashion communication. My turnaround story happened after I suffered a major disappointment in life. I was overlooked for promotion in office and this broke me deeply to an extent because, I worked really hard for it. It was at this point I came to the realization that the world isn't just going to hand you things simply because you deserve it even though you have worked hard for it. It is important that we learn to communicate our needs. However, in communicating our feelings we must also learn not to offend the people we are communicating with. It is one thing to be articulate. It is another thing to be offensive because in that process, you can equally end up isolating yourself from people.

Can you read someone's mind and tell what they are thinking? It is possible if you believe you can. You probably have done it before. You should, however, learn the difference between reading someone's mind and reading what you see. Many people confuse mind reading from analyzing your interaction. Mind reading essentially assumes that you know what they are thinking. You can get in their thoughts and predict what they are about to say.

This book is not about that. This book is about something tangible—what you can see in front of you. It is about making an informed decision about someone by evaluating their behavior, their demeanor, their speech patterns, and their appearance. It is about recognizing the many ways people communicate with you without saying a word. It is about listening to the message and reading deep between the lines to find the truth.

It is foolhardy to expect that people will always be honest with you. Honesty is not a virtue most people espouse. They will throw it out of the window at the earliest opportunity.

You have been in situations before where someone tried to take advantage of you. It might be a colleague, a friend or loved one, or even a stranger. That feeling of betrayal is disgusting. You feel terrible that someone thinks they can get away with it so easily. Worse still, it hurts if they did.

People use different means to try to get what they need from you. You might not realize it or like it, but it is the truth. In the corporate circle, as people work toward promotions and appraisals, in some cases, they have to win by all means, which could mean lying to you.

At home, your partner might be up to no good, but instead of confronting you about it and admitting their challenges, they tell convenient lies to conceal the problem. Everyone seems to have a reason why they lie. If you look at the reasons keenly, most of them are about selfishness. While you cannot be held responsible for someone else's selfishness or actions, you should hold yourself accountable for your indecision and gullibility.

Just because someone says something is true does not necessarily mean it is. You have a lot of tools and information at your disposal that you can use to confirm their statements. You have to learn to protect yourself by improving your awareness of the environment and the situations you get into.

The crux of this book is about reading people and analyzing them. However, you should not forget the important role you play in this dynamic. Before you analyze someone, learn about yourself. Recognize your inhibitions and your personal bias. These are some of the factors that influence decision-making.

How can you call someone out for lying when you probably do the same thing you are accusing them of all the time? While you might get away with such double standards once, over time, you become conflicted and cannot trust yourself to make the right judgment calls. It gets to a point where, instead of addressing the issues, you avoid them altogether because you feel guilty of doing the same thing you are castigating.

There are different levels of communication that go on around us. From the social circles we keep to our professional affiliations, it is important that you understand how the members of these circles communicate and the values you share. These values strengthen your relationships and are the reason why you are so close to one another. They also are the features you identify by, and without them, your interactions would be pointless.

Your ability to read someone is not always about what you can see. At times, it is also about what you feel when you are around them. Trust in your gut feeling. Many people ignore this. Gut feelings are a primal instinct that protects you from something or someone you are not comfortable with. When speaking to a liar, they might spin tales that have you wondering whether they are true or not. If you have a shred of doubt about it, it is highly likely you are right about them.

Identifying the different types of liars is another important technique that will save you a lot of trouble. Proximity to a sociopath is dangerous. They are unlike other liars you might come across. They feel nothing and show no remorse. They will never apologize and may actually enjoy your suffering from their lies, and they even goad you while at it. This is a dangerous person to be around. On the other hand, pathological and compulsive liars spin make-believe tales to suit their needs.

The best way to go about life is to be open to possibilities. Not all possibilities might be amazing, but in human interaction, it is always safe to expect the unexpected. Considering the different types of liars out there, you have to protect your space. Recognize that some people are beyond help, but suggest professional help for those who can benefit from it. It is painful when you have to distance yourself from people you love because you cannot trust them to tell you the truth.

That said, I hope that this book gives you everything that you desire and then some more. Here's to wonderful new beginnings!

Chapter 1 Benefits of Knowing How to Analyze People

We're inherently curious about why others think and feel the way they do. If a friend behaves unusually, we are quick to come up with theories about the motivations and intentions behind their bizarre actions. Some people even pride themselves on being an excellent judge of character. Unfortunately, we tend to rely solely on our past experiences and intuition when analyzing people, which can lead to incorrect assumptions. There needs to be a more precise way of interpreting the meaning behind the changes in a person's physiology. Learning the basics of how to systematically analyze what a person's body language says about their emotional state holds several benefits:

Gain More Confidence

If you can effectively learn to read other people's body language, gestures, and other nonverbal languages, then you can avoid getting confused or misunderstood what they are trying to express. It's a fact that most people get into a conflict because of miscommunication or misconception when relying on verbal communications.

A simple word can carry a lot of meanings and varying degrees and intensities. By merely relying on words, one can get confused, which can later lead a conflict to arise. However, since more than 55% of the ways people communicate are done through body language, then there is a lesser possibility for misunderstanding its usage compared when relating to words. And when you are sure that you can read people accurately, then this makes you more confident as you give them the right response at the quickest possible time since you don't need to linger your thoughts on things based on mere assumptions.

Control Social Situations

Humans are social beings, and there's no way around it. The desire to connect is within all of us, and it's also this desire that truly connects us all. Learning how to analyze others will enable you to understand them better on a deeper level. We are constantly broadcasting our identity through the way we present ourselves publicly. For example, the clothes we wear can say a lot about how we would like others to view us. Underneath these superficial qualities, there's information that is also sub-communicated about our identity without our conscious awareness. For example, how we dress may express how insecure we are about ourselves because we're trying to cover up the imperfections of our personality.

When you begin analyzing people, you'll notice that you start to uncover more interesting and more revealing information about others that's chiefly responsible for how they behave and feel. Possessing the ability to observe and interpret social cues will also better equip you to handle all types of interactions with tact and diplomacy. As you incorporate these tips and techniques, your relationships, both professional and personal, will flourish as you deepen your understanding of the universal language of humans that is body language.

As of late, there's been an epidemic of self-proclaimed socially awkward people in the last decade. The current era of Facebook, text messaging, and Snapchat has shaped the way an entire generation has developed socially. That's not to say that they have been stunted in their social development. Communicating through these new mediums is the quickest, most convenient way for us to express our social selves. However, when we communicate through these new mediums that solely rely on words, we lose the non-verbal aspects of communication. Also, unlike with non-verbal communication, we can easily lie with our words.

Even in this digital age of shopping for groceries on Amazon, there are still some activities that require us to have face-to-face interactions. In a world filled with people who are more accustomed to typing or texting behind a screen, learning how to analyze body language would give you a huge advantage in social situations. So until absolutely everything can be accomplished from the comfort of your home without speaking to another human being, it's an excellent investment to work on your social intelligence.

Better Relationships

Being in a relationship is not easy, especially when most of the time, we fail to read each other accurately and when emotional energies don't synchronize. However, when you can read and analyze other people, you can quickly tell when someone is interested in you, and your date can go well because you are entirely in rapport with each other. When it comes to a more serious relationship, clearly reading your loved one will give you a deeper understanding of his thoughts and actions; thus, it will be easier for you to communicate effectively with him.

More often than not, relationships are broken because of miscommunication, but if you can both read and analyze each other's behavior, you can prevent a deep misunderstanding which often leads to separation.

Relationships need trust and understanding along with open communication, and people tend to close up and refuse to tell what they are experiencing when they're hurt, angry, or anxious. It is only through having the ability to read clearly without those things that tend to cloud your thoughts and emotions will you be able to prevent a misunderstanding from getting in the way of your relationship.

Increase Emotional Intelligence

After learning how to read the body language of the people around you, you'll naturally begin to become more self-conscious of your body language. It can be a bit overwhelming to comprehend how the smallest of actions can expose how we feel at any given moment. This idea that there are people equipped with the ability to read anyone's minds just by looking at them practically would make anyone feel extremely vulnerable.

The best course of action would be to take measures to control our body's physiology to convey to others how we want to be perceived. This requires us to be self-aware enough to know when we're sliding back into our default body language and then modifying it to portray ourselves the way we would like to be portrayed. You'll begin to recognize that our emotions can be influenced by how we position our bodies. The idea of deliberately placing ourselves in socially dominant stances to feel more self-confident has become a popular theory in the last decade.

Stances such as "The Wonder Woman," which require one to spread their feet a little wider than shoulder-width apart and place their hands on their hips, can make a person feel just as powerful and confident as the Amazonian heroine herself. When we modify the way we stand, we are proactive in managing our emotions. The truth is, so many of us allow our emotions to control our lives that we forget that we have emotions and that we are not our emotions.

By changing how we feel internally, it can transform our thoughts, beliefs, and behavior. To produce lasting changes, manipulating your body language as an emotional management technique requires diligence and practice, especially to turn this skill into a habit. At first, it'll take an overwhelming amount of effort to monitor our emotions since we haven't been conditioned to manage them. One way to accelerate this process is to integrate it into our social life to the point where it becomes our natural way of reacting to the world. It's easy to regulate your emotions when you're alone. It's much more challenging to practice this in the company of your friends and family.

Sometimes, our friends and family may say or do things that we don't agree with. It's not our responsibility to change these things about them, but we are always responsible for how we emotionally react to them. If you keep tabs on your feelings at any given moment and dissociate yourself from them in the toughest of scenarios, you'll make smarter decisions and take more deliberate action.

More Opportunity for Success

When you have learned to master the skillful art of reading people's body language, you are also capable of winning relationships as you can quickly establish rapport with people. Being able to build good relationships with others will open up more opportunities for you in all aspects of your life, particularly in business or career, which is scoreboards of success. Recognize that people in the industry want to deal and give favor to people they want. Job interviewers are most likely to favor people who emit a positive body language than people to send them negative body cues.

Spotting Deception

Everybody lies; the question is, how can we recognize when people lie before we suffer the consequences of their dishonesty? The ability to read people and figure out when they're lying is the closest thing to a superpower you can wield. All it takes is to learn what to look out for in a person's body language and hone your observation skills, so you notice the signs every time they occur. The majority of the population is not aware that their dishonesty can be broadcasted publicly by their bodies. However skilled you may be at lying, it takes a lot of work for the brain to lie. We essentially need to hold on to two realities in our head, the reality of truth, and the reality we've conjured with our lies. It reaches a point where the brain is too preoccupied to ensure that the body's communication is in agreement with your lie, so it carelessly places your body on autopilot. Your body acts as an inadvertent tattletale when you lie while trying to ensure nobody knows that you're lying.

An example of this is when somebody is unable to maintain eye contact. When a person displays this type of behavior, there's a slight possibility that they are not telling the truth. This is the body's way of protecting itself from those who can potentially "punish" the individual if they're caught lying. If the eyes are the windows to the soul, constantly breaking eye contact suggests that your soul has something to hide. Of course, other factors need to be considered. Sometimes, the body fails to suppress certain behavioral tics that indicate that what you're saying may not be in harmony with the truth. For example, if your coworker compliments the way you've dressed for work, but the facial muscles used for frowning slightly twitch, this may indicate that they are disingenuous with their compliment.

This example brings up the question of whether every lie is "sinister" and if you should expose every attempt at deceit you encounter. Would it be so terrible to go about your day believing that someone expressed a positive interest in the way you dress? Not at all! Some may prefer to live a life of blissful ignorance and wouldn't prefer to peek behind the curtain for fear that they'll regret learning the truth. This book will provide you with the tools to enable you to decide instead of letting others decide whether you deserve to hear the truth. There may not be any urgency to spot "white lies," such as insincere compliments. However, there is an urgency to be equipped with this skill if a person's dishonesty can have drastic consequences if not addressed immediately. When you can recognize the signs that somebody may be lying to you, the social dynamics of your interactions will shift in your favor when dealing with people with hidden agendas.

Chapter 2 Body Language Basics

One of the easiest ways to analyze other people is to look at their body language. How a person holds themselves, moves, and even speaks can tell you a lot about them. Everyone has plenty of variation between their mannerisms, and there's no exact way to tell what makes up a person. There are still many similar indications among groups of people that can give you a deep insight into how someone functions.

It's not easy because it starts with becoming aware of your own body language. In order to understand and attempt to overcome the enigma that is body language, you have to be hyper aware.

Some people might be more aware of their movements than they are their thoughts. Women are likely going to be more aware of their bodies and the space they take up, mostly because of the patriarchal society we grew up in. Everyone still might find difficulty in confronting the way they hold their body. You can lose focus while trying to maintain awareness, becoming too insecure about your own body and movements.

Once you get to know the body movements of another person better, you can also understand what makes them unique. The more you know about a person, the better you can conclude the best strategy for persuasion.

Cultural Differences

Every person is different, and sometimes, how one person holds their body has a different meaning than someone who stands the same way. There are plenty of ways that a person's body language differs, so it's important to remember that not everything about a certain body movement is 100 percent true for every person. This is crucial to remember when talking to people from different cultural backgrounds.

There are some cultures that practice modesty, so touching might be completely off limits. Other cultures might be more open to expressing their feelings through their bodies. So culture is important to remember when thinking about how a person might use their body.

Studying Others' Movements

Once you become more aware of body movements and what they might represent, you can start studying them when interacting with different people. Everyone you come in contact with uses their body to represent different things. Some people are closed off, and others might be more open. These are some small differences you could tell just by observing someone's body language.

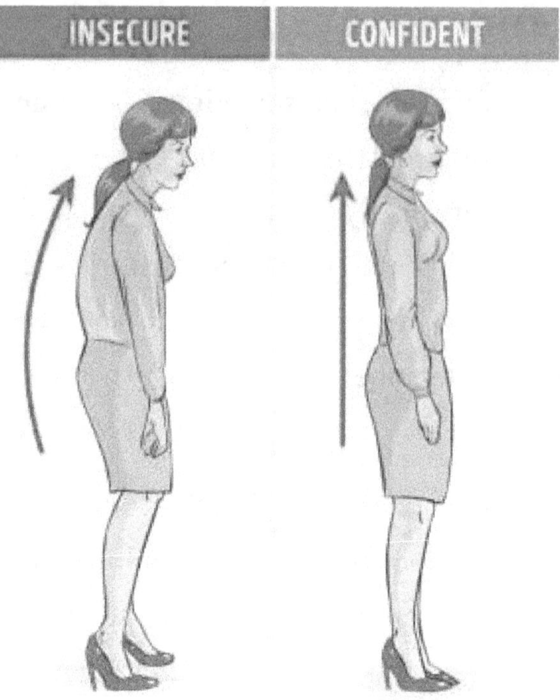

When studying other people and yourself, it's important to try and act naturally as well. It can be easy to become hyper-aware of your movements but know that you don't have to hold your body a certain way. Not everyone is as aware of body movements as others might be, so at the end of the day, don't look into your own movements too much.

Still, once you start studying others' body movements, you'll start to realize how much you can get to know them. Certain things might all start to make sense after meeting a variety of individuals. You might notice that one of your friends is rather pretentious in the way they hold themselves or talk. Other friends might show how insecure they are with themselves, even though you thought they had been incredibly confident since you'd known them.

Knowing a person's body language and having insight as to why they might move a certain way can allow you to understand them at their core better. This gives you greater leverage when it comes to persuading them. You might want to match the confidence of your boss when striking up a deal for a raise. Perhaps you noticed you need to be more relaxed around certain friends that seem to be shy or nervous. Becoming aware of your body language can be scary at first, but eventually, you'll be comfortable with the way you move.

To start practicing being comfortable with your own body, try hanging out in front of a mirror. When you're eating dinner, watching TV, or even lounging in bed, set up a mirror so you can see how you hold yourself. Once you get an outsider's perspective of how you move, you'll be able to see how others move as well.

Eye Contact

Eye contact is one of the biggest clues you can use to determine how someone truly is. It's important to become aware of your own use of eye contact as well because it gives others clues about your personality and true nature. Maintaining eye contact is important to let a person know that you're attentive to what they are talking about.

It can also be overused, however, and let people know that you're trying too hard to convince them that you're listening. Too much eye contact can sometimes intimidate others as well, so if you notice that a person is getting nervous because of the amount of eye contact you're having with them, change it up every now and then.

Pupil dilation can be a direct indication that a person is interested in what you're saying. Studies have proven that when the pupils of a person whom you are making eye contact with begin dilating, it means they are interested in what you have to say. They are listening to you with their utmost attention, and they're thinking deeply about what you're saying. You know when a person's pupils are dilated while talking to you that they are legitimately interested in the conversation.

Shifty eyes will indicate the opposite. Someone who is looking at your eyes back and forth is probably trying to convince you that they are listening. They are aware that they need to try and make eye contact, but they are completely zoned out with what you are saying. Those with shifty eyes might also be lying to you or trying to deceive you in some way. They might be having difficulty maintaining eye contact with you because they know they are deceitful.

Mouth Movements

What someone does with their mouth is very crucial to understanding their personality as well. Someone with tight or pursed lips might be trying to concentrate, or they also might be trying hard to hide a sour face. You can analyze a person's smile as well. If the corners of their eyes aren't creased, they might be forcing a smile with you.

Someone that's faking a smile isn't necessarily evil; they might just be thinking of something else, too diverted to give their full focus to what you're saying. Sometimes, smiles are also reactions to uncomfortable situations.

When monkeys smile, it's not because they are happy, but mostly because they are showing their teeth as a way of threatening those around them. When they feel scared and nervous, they'll open their mouths wide, showing that they have teeth they could use to hurt. The same goes for dogs. They only show their teeth when they are feeling threatened. For humans, this can be true sometimes as well, but on a subconscious level.

Nervous laughing and smiling are just a way for a person to alleviate their tension. You can tell someone is genuinely smiling when they have creases in the corners of their eyes.

A person that is continually covering their mouth also is usually nervous. They might bite their lip, finger, or put a fist over their mouth. Knowing when a person is uncomfortable or nervous can sometimes be helpful when trying to persuade them.

Nodding

How a person turns and tilts their head can be a subtle movement. In most cases, people aren't aware when they are moving their head around. The neck and head movements of the person you're talking to can give you great insight into what they might be thinking on a deeper level.

Someone that nods their head rather quickly while listening to you might just be anxious, by trying to move the conversation along as quickly as possible. They're attempting to set a pace for you so that you speak faster. They want to let you know they hear you, but you're not speaking fast enough. If someone is doing this to you, try to speed up your words in order to hold their attention.

Someone who tilts their head to the side might have a legitimate interest in what you're saying. They are attempting to turn an ear towards you, so they can hear you better, whether they're aware of their movements or not. They also are indicating to you that they hear you and they want you to keep talking. It's a way for them to get closer to you in the conversation without having to make any interjections or interruptions.

If someone is nodding too artificially, they might just be attempting to convince you that they are interested in what you are saying. They could be aware that they should be paying attention, but they might have lost interest. In an attempt to keep up, they pretend to nod their head. They also might not understand what you're saying, so they nod to make you think they're keeping up. If you notice others around you are artificially nodding their head, it'd be worth it to either change the subject to regain attention or explain yourself better as they might just be confused.

Mimicking someone's head movements can be very helpful in using persuasion. A gentle tilt of the head while listening to them can show that you are comprehending what they're saying. It can also show that you're empathetic to them, especially if they seem to be talking about something that is hard for them.

Hands and Arms

How someone uses their hands and arms is another way that body language can be interpreted to get a better understanding of the people you're interacting with. Our hands represent so much about ourselves. They're a way of expressing stories, putting different emphasis on various parts. If someone's telling a story, they're going to use hand gestures to keep people interested. Think of someone engaged in a conversation as someone that's directing an orchestra. They'll lift their hands to keep up a rhythm and pace for those listening.

Someone's hands and arms can also express how open or closed off they are. They can be like the doorway into someone's body. If they're crossed tightly in front of someone's chest, that person might be a little more closed off, not wanting to engage too much in conversation. Having their arms crossed doesn't always mean that someone is necessarily closed off. They might also just be wanting to rest their arms, so if they're loosely hanging in front of their chest, they're likely just casually listening to you.

Someone that has their arms outstretched, maybe over their head, will likely be very open and possibly even trying to exert power over a situation. Someone with their hands on their hips might also be trying to assert their power.

Signals

Everyone has different body language cues that they use as signals. Between cultures, genders, and ages, different movements someone makes with their bodies can be conscious or subconscious signals that they're giving to the people around them. Signals let other people know bits of information without having to say anything at all.

Someone with their arms crossed, eyes fading on a couch at a party is giving the signal that they're likely ready to head home for the night. Someone else on that couch could be sitting on the edge of their seat, laughing loudly, signaling they're not going to be heading to bed anytime soon.

Signals help the people around the signaler know things that they might not easily be able to express with their bodies. Some are very good at picking up on other people's signals, and some people struggle to understand those around them.

When it comes to trying to persuade someone, there are some crucial signals that a person will need to be able to lead a conversation properly.

Starting a Conversation

Next time you're sitting quietly in a room with another person, wait until they start the conversation to speak. This will allow you to study how they might start a conversation. Most people will give some sort of signal with their body that they are about to begin speaking. They might clear their throat, turn their head, adjust their shirt, or shift in their seat. There is usually something, no matter how small it might be, that a person does right before they start a conversation.

Starting a conversation, especially one that is meant to persuade another person, is important for laying the groundwork for your argument. No one is going to want to give their full attention to someone that is struggling to start. If you're nervous and jumping over your words right off the bat, it's going to be much harder to keep up.

Leading the Conversation

The moment a conversation begins, it can be tricky to maintain the right amount of back and forth. You avoid being too pushy, at the same time, you also don't want to let them talk too much, not allowing you anytime to state your points. If you feel like the other party isn't letting you talk enough, there are obvious phrases you can use to speak your mind. You might try saying something like, "can I just say…," "could I speak for a minute?" or "I'm listening but can I say something really quick?"

These can be hard to say in some situations, and some people might even perceive you as being rude if you make a large interjection. What your best option might be is to use your body to redirect focus. Put your hands on your hips or tilt your head to let the other person know that you have something to say. Try leaning in to let them know that you want to take over as the leader of your current conversation.

Leading the conversation can be tricky because no one wants to listen to someone that is interrupting them. It's still important that you get your turn to speak as well. There are ways you can practice leading conversations so that when it comes time to have an important persuasion, you can properly lead. Next time you want to say something, don't. Instead, let the other person continue speaking and interject later. Sometimes we get so anxious to say our part we distract from the true conversation, invalidating any argument we have to the person that we interrupted.

An alternative way to practice leading the conversation is to speak up the next time you want to say something. If you have something to say, but you would rather just keep quiet, force yourself to say what you want. These two methods of practice will give you two alternate perspectives on leading a conversation that you might not get otherwise.

Chapter 3 How Your Body Language Affects You

Believe it or not, how you use your body can directly affect how you function as well. There are ways that you can use to improve how you think and the capacity of your memory just by the way that you use your hands and arms. Not only are there physical differences in terms of how you use your body, but you will also be affected by the way others perceive you.

If you're constantly closed off, always crossing your arms, there are probably a lot of people that might not open up or talk to you because they assume you have no interest in a conversation. If you're always very open with your body, exerting confidence and holding yourself high, others might end up being intimidated by you. You might not have any intention of closing others off or being intimidating, but your body can show that in ways that your mouth doesn't.

There are other ways that your own body language can actually mentally affect you.

Open Your Mind

Someone that starts opening their arms when they talk will begin to let others know that they are much more open-minded. If you stand with arms open, or just hanging relaxed by your side, you let the people around you know that you are confident and willing to talk with them about different things.

While having open arms is a signal for others, it's also a signal for your brain. Studies show that by standing with open arms verses crossed ones, you can actually signal your brain to be more open. You'll start to think of new ideas that you wouldn't if you kept your arms crossed. The same applies to the rest of your body. The more open you are with your movements, the more you allow your brain to have different ideas.

Improve Your Memory

Those that talk with their hands also tends to have a better memory than those that don't. Using your hands can put physical reminders in your brain for ideas and thoughts that you might be discussing. If you mimic numbers or shapes when you're talking about different ideas, especially in a business setting, not only will you remember what you're discussing better, but those around you will find your story more memorable as well.

Using your hands to talk while telling a story will also help you remember the things that you went through. You're encouraging your brain to continue thinking, and keeping your arms open will open up your brain to new thoughts and feelings you might not have had should you have spoken with your arms crossed and closed off.

Verbal Cues

While there are many things that a person can say with their body, there are many more things that they can say with their mouth. There's a seemingly limitless amount of languages out there, as each specific language has many subparts. Think of how many different accents there might be in just New York City. As we continue to develop and blend different cultures and languages, only more will develop. It's hard to keep up with what we already know, but there are ways to still pick up on others' meaning without having to memorize every word in the dictionary.

Just because a person says a certain word, doesn't indicate that they actually mean what they say.

Knowing why people say the things they do can be one of the trickiest codes to try and crack. You don't always have to know what a person means in order to understand what they're trying to say. You can pick up on what a person's intention is by listening to how they talk and mixing that with their body language. It's important to read someone's mood so you don't say the wrong thing or anything that could potentially change the direction of the conversation.

Next time you find something on TV that's in a different language than any you can speak, try watching without subtitles. You'll be surprised to see that you actually understand part of the storyline. Don't look at what they're saying, but how they're saying it. Is there pain in their eyes? Do they look happy or sad? Sometimes if you can't understand what a person is saying, maybe because the room is loud or they're speaking softly, try looking into their eyes. You might get a sense of what they're saying if you just watch the words their mouth is attempting to put together.

There are certain specific cues that someone can give when they're trying to direct a conversation. When you're trying to persuade someone, you might want to try and use different keywords to help you in leading the conversation. Some people get too hung up on the actual words someone is saying when they should just be trying to listen to the message they're getting across.

It can seem difficult to try to crack what someone else means, but it can be done. Think about your pets. You can tell if your dog is sad, sleepy, hungry, or in a playful mood, but you don't have actual conversations with them. Sometimes you can analyze what a person is saying best by figuring out the noises they're making rather than dissecting every word that they say.

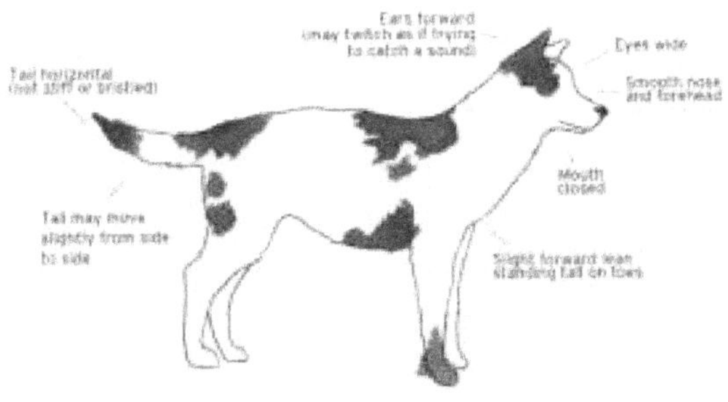

Emphasis Cues

When trying to persuade someone, you're going to want to have a pretty good argument already prepared in order to build your case. You might want to include some emphasis cues when you're speaking. It can be hard to incorporate these phrases naturally, but it's good to practice so you can become a better persuader.

"This is important," "you need to know," "let me explain," are all phrases that grab the attention of the person that you're speaking to. You might start to notice others' emphasis cues better after reading this section as well. You should be listening, and using in your own speech, phrases that seem to emphasize an important part of a conversation.

Sometimes, these emphasis cues aren't even actual phrases. They might just be verbal indications that something is important, such as someone raising their voice when talking about an important part of their argument. They also might repeat the word several times or stop for a pause for the listener to digest what they just said. Emphasis cues are important to understand to get a better grasp of what might be important to an individual. If you listen to what they're emphasizing, you'll be able to also formulate your thoughts and arguments around the things that are important to them.

Organizational Cues

"First, second, third," "to summarize," "the topic is," are all phrases that could be considered organizational cues. These cues help a person indicate that they are trying to organize their thoughts, again, maybe putting emphasis on the things that are the most important.

Organizational cues are important for you to use in your arguments in persuasions in order to get people on your side. You want them to understand that you're attentive to what they have to say and that they should be listening to you. You're trying to formulate a plan based on both your thoughts and opinions and not just the words of one specific individual.

Organizational cues allow the speaker to put emphasis on what's important while also maintaining a clear thought and direct focus. Organizational cues might not be phrases either. It could just be someone clearing their throat, redirecting the conversation back to a previous topic, or stopping in order for everyone to collect their thoughts.

Watch Your Pitch

Pitch is an important key when trying to direct one's conversation in their favor. Pitch is the level of your voice, and the overall sound quality. Someone with a deep pitch might have a more soothing tone, while someone with a high-pitched voice might make their listeners more alert. Not everyone can help the natural pitch of their voice. There are some people that have extremely low voices that are hard to hear, and some people just have naturally shrill voices that seem as though they bother everyone around them!

While your natural pitch can't always be controlled, you can at least help direct that pitch towards a more productive tone in order to keep your listeners engaged with what you have to say. Many of us let our pitch become too high and whiny when we are in professional settings, trying to keep our dictation sharp. If you feel like your voice is becoming high and shrill, don't be afraid to stop, clear your throat, and start again. The people around you will likely be grateful that you're adjusting your tone for their listening pleasure.

Be careful not to let the end of your voice go up when speaking. Many people, especially when talking on a phone, tend to let the end of their words go up like they're asking a question. This kind of speaking is also common among those that might be giving a speech. They'll say a phrase very clearly with dictation, but they'll also end the sentence in a high pitched way as if they're asking a question. This is something that should be avoided in order to keep the attention of your listeners.

It's important to find your optimal pitch. Some people have very soft voices that can be hard to hear. In this situation, it's important to practice speaking up when it's necessary. Someone that tends to speak loudly should try talking low as often as possible to help balance their pitch out. The greatest way to practice is alone, and to record what you're saying. You don't want to analyze the way you speak too deeply, but practicing always helps, especially for those that find difficulty in speaking their views.

It's also important to have a confident pitch to let others know they should listen to you. Someone that's always talking timidly or like they're asking a question will let the others around them assume that what they have to say isn't interesting. If you're so unsure of what you're saying, why should someone else listen to you? The best way to ensure others are paying attention is to make sure that you speak with confidence.

Listen to Others

Talking about yourself can elicit the same good feelings that money and food cause. We like talking about ourselves more than we enjoy listening to other people talk about themselves for the most part. While it can seem selfish, it's true that most people would prefer to talk about themselves. This means that when conversing with other people, you should avoid talking about yourself too much.

You don't want to make the conversation completely about other people, but no one will pay attention if the only thing you talk about is yourself. Giving advice can also be helpful, but people generally don't engage as often with those that offer too much advice, especially when it isn't asked for.

Listening to other people can actually be challenging for some. They might find it difficult not to let their mind wander, especially if the other person is talking too much about themselves. Some people will find that they're usually forming their next thought while the other person is talking, instead of actually listening to them. If you find your mind wandering when someone else is talking, redirect your thoughts back to their words. Don't just listen to what they're saying. Watch how they're saying it. Listen to their voice and look into their eyes. People will notice whether or not you're listening to them. Even if they aren't skilled in body language, they will still be able to at least sense that you might not be fully engaged as well.

Don't just put an emphasis on listening to others. Make the conversation about them as well. Ask questions about the person, in an attempt to get to know them better. You'll find that people usually like to answer questions about themselves. This is often a technique you'll see in many salespeople. They'll ask where you got your shirt, or if you've had a good day. This is to get the person thinking about themselves, and they'll usually end up opening up a bit more to the salesperson as well.

People don't like to be corrected. While it can be hard to avoid sometimes, most people don't want to be interrupted to be told that they were wrong. Most people will respect you much more if you just let them talk rather than trying to prove them wrong. This is very important to remember, especially when trying to persuade and analyze others.

Talk about "we," not "you." If you're trying to make suggestions, maybe to a spouse or friend about an improvement in their lifestyle, use "we" instead. Don't say, "you should try waking up earlier on the weekends," say, "we should get up early on Sunday and go on a walk together!" People will respond much better to suggestions if you include yourself.

Apologizing

It can be hard to apologize, especially for those with high levels of pride, but it's important in gaining the respect of the people around you. If you apologize for being late rather than giving every explanation you can, most will respond much better to this than if you were to try to make yourself look better with excuses.

They also like to see humility, and that you maybe aren't afraid to express yourself. If you can open up with someone and just say, "I'm sorry I didn't respond to your text, I was just having a really bad day," they'll usually be very forgiving rather than if you would've just blown them off.

However, don't apologize too much. It can lead others not to trust you. Sometimes we have the urge to apologize for things that were out of our control in an attempt to make ourselves look better.

If you have to apologize after every little thing you say, why should anyone listen to you in the first place? Next time you feel the urge to apologize for something that was out of your control, try saying thank you instead. After having a long conversation with a friend, don't say, "Sorry you had to listen to me rant!" Instead, try something like, "Thank you for being such a great listener. I'm glad to have a friend like you!" People will generally respond much more positively to a thankful person than someone that always invalidates themselves. You'll find that you start to treat yourself much better if you stick to this method of apology as well.

The Power of Your Body

Our bodies have so much power, and not just with how much we're able to lift or carry. Physical strength is important, but even the weakest of people can control a room with their body movements alone.

We can't get into every specific detail of what someone's physical actions might be trying to convey, but the framework for how to analyze those movements is there. Once you understand how someone else might be using their body to persuade others, you can start to work on your own skills of persuasion.

There are many ways that someone can use their body to convince others to do what they want, but it won't always work on everyone. Some people respond to sexual persuasion while others are repulsed by the thought. Some people respond to a physical threat from those that seem stronger than them, but others might be ready for the fight.

There are multiple ways that you can use your body to persuade others without being sexual or physically intimidating. Keeping your body open and visible is crucial in letting others know they can trust you. Try making sure to remove physical barriers that might keep you separated from the person you're talking to. Step around a chair or table that's blocking you from making a full connection with the person you're trying to talk to.

This also shows that you're confident and interested in speaking your mind while hearing what the other person has to say as well. When analyzing other people's movements, you can also figure out what things you can do yourself to be more confident. Study certain celebrities to see how they hold themselves in various scenarios. Everyone has their own movements, but mimicking others can still help you find your own footing when it comes to having a persuasive demeanor overall.

Smiling is Important

Our smiles are one of the most powerful tools we've been given. You can turn any situation from bad to good just by turning up the corners of your mouth. Some people feel that if they don't have straight teeth or smiles that are bright white, they aren't worth anything. Even those that don't have all their teeth can have much more beautiful smiles than someone that's spent thousands on dental work.

A smile isn't just about what teeth you're showing. It's a way to engage another person. Most people will smile if someone else smiles at them first. If they do smile, they'll end up having a better mood overall.

Chapter 4 What Is Verbal Communication?

Verbal communication is based on an interaction model in which signs are used to elaborate a message. This definition may sound technical, but it simply refers to the letters, syllables, and words understood as signs, and to their different unions to elaborate complete messages, that other people are capable of understanding and interpreting.

When we talk about oral communication, we usually think of a person who articulates a speech. However, there are two forms of verbal communication:

Oral communication: Includes words verbalized by means of voice and words spoken in a gestural way. For example, in sign language.

Written communication: It is done through written messages that the receiver must read and interpret.

Oral communication is framed in a specific situation that will be decisive for the effectiveness of the message. All these elements must be taken into account in order to construct appropriate messages in form and content.

Issuer: This is the person who generates the message.

Recipient: Is the person who receives the message and interprets it.

Message: The content, the information that goes from the sender to the receiver.

Code: System that we use to articulate the message, usually we identify it with the language.

Channel: Medium through which the message is transmitted.

Context: General situation in which verbal communication is framed.

This simple scheme is what will determine the effectiveness of our communication.

The Importance of Verbal Communication in Work Groups

In any methodology that includes working groups, communication is fundamental. Verbal communication is immediate. That's why we use it continuously both to organize groups internally and to exchange messages between different workgroups.

The dynamism and effectiveness of the groups depend on communication. A Scrum process, for example, would be unfeasible without a shared model of communication, and its development is very difficult if verbal communication is deficient.

As we say, communicative analysis tends to focus on most occasions on non-verbal communication. However, functional communication, the one we use continuously and the one that carries the information load is verbal, and therefore we must master it.

Improve Verbal Communication in Our Day to Day

Actually, verbal communication requires a long process of improvement, but we will highlight some aspects that we can improve simply by being aware of our daily verbal messages.

Avoid snitches and phrases. These are very common when you start sentences and they occur unconsciously.

Modulate the tone of your voice. The volume of your message will be based on the message and the environment in which you find yourself.

Pauses and active listening should be part of all your verbal interactions. So important as to what is expressed and what is not said.

Communicate naturally, sometimes adopting certain tones or attitudes makes the defects of oral communication more evident.

You must be clear and precise at all times, regardless of who the recipient is. Two personal traits should accompany our messages: passion (naturally) and education.

Use if possible, the name of your interlocutor, this creates confidence. These are some tips that you can use whether you have to prepare a speech or your day-to-day work environment.

Now we know the importance of speech and oratory, so we prepare specific courses focused on this subject if you want more information contact us.

It is through the study of body language and non-verbal intelligence that we can read and interpret clues.

Chapter 5 How to Interpret Verbal Communication

A young student has worked over 20 hours to complete a 40-page essay for her college class. She then had to develop a visual representation to accompany her presentation. After three restless nights and countless cups of coffee, she is finally ready to present her finished report to the class. After performing an engaging and educational discourse, she breathed a deep sigh of relief. After class, she approached her professor and asked him how he enjoyed it. Barely looking up from his computer, the professor stopped and said, "It was fine," in a monotone voice. She was devastated. After dedicating all of her time and resources to this project, she was not satisfied with, "It was fine." A week later, after wondering what she could have improved upon, she finally got her grade back. Shaking, she opened the link and saw a 100% grade. She was ecstatic. She felt greatly accomplished and proud of her work. However, she still wondered why the professor gave her that response if he was going to give her an A.

The professor could have genuinely loved her presentation. In fact, it could have given him chills. However, because he was so monotone in his response, the student grew insecure. He gave off the impression that he did not appreciate all of her hard work. In reality, the professor greatly enjoyed it; so much so, he gave her a perfect grade. What is the issue with his actions?

Likely, you would conclude that the way he uttered, "It was fine," was a turn off. That monotone delivery is quite different from the excited, "It was fine!" paired with a clap. This is the power of verbal communication. Although one person may say one thing, the way they speak it reveals the truth. Our body language works closely with the manner in which we speak. A rather rude comment can be overlooked when paired with a smiling face, or it could be taken as extremely creepy. In addition, a smile can hide insidious intentions. This is why body language is a compilation of various components.

When a person constantly speaks in a harsh, assertive, and bold manner, others may conclude that that person is angry. They may even avoid associating with them for fear of embracing negative energy. In reality, the person could be amicable and positive. However, the way they place great emphasis on certain words or topics is intimidating. The power of tone, emphasis, and volume can create great conclusions when it comes to reputation. However, there are exceptions to this theory. Some individuals may express themselves one way, yet their actual personality is quite different. Take, for example, the late Michael Jackson. Michael had an extremely light and timid voice. He would speak almost like an unsure child, retelling a bedtime story. Upon only hearing him, one may conclude that Michael was submissive, shy, and quiet. The reality of his persona was quite different. The innovation found within his music and the creativity exuded through his dance moves illuminated great power and confidence. Despite the volume, tone, and inflection of his voice, he was a mighty lion when it came to his craft. Personal friends and family members, however, knew that somewhere, deep inside, lived a submissive, shy, and quiet person. This denotes that within our voice, despite intention, lie deep-rooted personality traits that we may be blind to. The loud and boisterous individual may be seeking to compensate for a deep insecurity. The arrogant and assertive lawyer may be fuming with angry emotions. The way in which a person speaks is complex and reveals truth.

The power behind how you say something can turn your innovative idea into a passed opportunity. Imagine pitching an idea for a new innovation with a monotone voice and no sign of excitement. Surely, those on the other end would not be convinced this is your passion. You may have missed your opportunity simple because you lacked enthusiasm. Your voice can also be a manipulative tool used to assert to others. There is a stark distinction between yelling rules and explaining them. The way a person says something can make a difference in how the sentence is perceived. A stressed manager can assert, "Why are you always late?" to an employee with a stern voice and a frowning mouth. Or she could kindly say, "Why are you always late?" with a slight touch on the shoulder and a concerned tone. This could be the moment where the employee either opens up or seeks further employment. When you think about it, words are just extensions of the mind. We all use them and express ourselves in one way or the other. However, the tone can drastically alter our perceived intentions and even our reputation.

The volume in which one speaks can ignite action. A whisper may indicate confidential information, while a loud yelp could signal, "Get away." In addition, a monotone voice could indicate disinterest where an emphasis on words and syllables could signal excitement. Sarcasm, on the other hand, is quite tricky to decode as it is subjective to the person speaking. One lively individual could show sarcasm in the same manner they would offer a greeting. This is where contextual clues come into play. Analyze the person's body language. Do they have a slight smile or a straight face? Does what they say seem outlandish in relation to the topic at hand? Interpreting sarcasm involves integrative techniques to understanding. It is a complex system that is unique to each person. One of the primary reasons why sarcasm is so difficult to understand for some is because it can mimic traditional body language cues. In this respect, it may be essential to get to know the person you are speaking with, so they can better understand your personality. Then, little by little, bring on the sarcasm!

Understanding your personal inflection can affect your reputation. You may have the purest of intentions, but your diction, volume, and choice of words is taken adversely. Others may create a distance between themselves and you due to this inconsistency. Being cognizant of the way you say something can be a true indicator of your intention. In addition, your communication skills will operate smoothly. The two main components of mastering effective communication are control and awareness. It is important to control the tone, inflection, and volume of your voice. It may even be necessary to control the type of words you use. Next, being aware of your audience, surroundings, and mood can play a huge role in how your words come off. A bad or melancholy mood may not be suitable for a children's book reading at the library. You can practice altering your verbal skills by seeking feedback from others. Have them analyze how you express a sentence, and they can provide constructive ways to improve.

Chapter 6 What is Non-Verbal Communication

Non-verbal communication is anything that does not have to do with your speech. When you communicate non-verbally, you are doing so with your body language. Non-verbal communication is older than history. It is the most primitive type of communication around. Animals may not have a complex language to go off of like we do, but they are still very much able to communicate with other people. This is why non-verbal communication will be where we start. You need a good handle on what people say with their bodies before you get into the much trickier topic of what they are trying to say with their voice.

Body language is a much better indicator of a person's true feelings towards an event that is taking place or toward the people in the room. You can pretty easily hide your true feelings with your voice and say the right words to brush it all away. However, there will always be tip-offs related to how you are moving your body.

Movement is the biggest part of communication. You need to keep an eye on everything from the person's hands to their eyes, feet, up to their chest. It can feel a little overwhelming. This is a lot of information to take in and not a whole lot of time to master it. If you feel like you are a little overwhelmed, just keep in mind that you already have a solid background in this. You have been communicating with others and reading their communications, both verbally and non-verbally, your entire life.

Keying into non-verbal communication allows you to read people silently. Even if the person is not speaking to you or you cannot hear them, you can still figure out what their general disposition is. Being able to silently read people is an incredible talent.

These are all things you know subconsciously. You just need to bring that all to the surface and begin to understand the inner workings of these things. Do not feel discouraged by all of the information. You bought this book so that you could not only read it but also keep it as a reference as you make your way through the world of analyzing people. None of this information is going to stick with you immediately.

Knowing your audience is a huge part of making friends and making sure they stay as your friends. It is also a large part of keeping people, even those you do not happen to know, interested and engaged with what you are saying. If you are going to address a crowd, for example, you need to know how to read the room and figure out how to tackle your speech or toast.

It is vastly easier to do once you have a solid handle on cold and speed reading.

We all know how nerve-wracking it can be to have to face groups of people. Nobody wants to put themselves in a situation where they are in front of a large crowd of other human beings who are all just waiting for them to slip up. That is how it feels, anyway.

However, there is a certain kind of stress being one-on-one with somebody can bring. Reading a room is great, but knowing your audience is not just about rooms of people. It is also about being able to figure out whether you are aiming to please the person you are talking to, or whether they are not going to like or pick up on your message. This is why you need to understand non-verbal communication–it helps you to key in on the person's needs.

Everybody needs something different. Depending on our personality types, whether you are looking at the Myer-Briggs or a different form of categorization, there will be different styles on how you tackle conversation. Some people will be receptive to you joking around with them and adding humor into your approach. Others will be better suited to a serious conversation with a point-blank premise laid out clearly before them. It depends on the person; that is why reading them is so necessary.

Principles of Nonverbal Communication

When thinking about the principles of nonverbal communication, it is not exactly what you state, it is the way you state it. The tone with which you convey your words, the manner in which you stand, and the exceptionally significant eye to eye connection association express information that words cannot. The best individuals are not simply incredible scholars or innovative scribes, they know the nuances of exhibiting trust in their nonverbal communication, ordering the consideration of everybody around them.

How might you ace this craftsmanship? Here are three hints to kick you off:

Find your capacity position.

Your stance is a piece of your communication arms stockpile and can motion toward other individuals how you are feeling or thinking. In the event that you are standing, a great power position resembles: feet shoulder-width separated, hands at your sides, bears back and head up. On the off chance that you are sitting, it would seem that: feet solidly on the ground, straight back and head up.

In either case, keeping your back straight back and bears wide will likewise enable you to extend your voice so others can hear you. Obviously, remain somewhat free in these stances to abstain from looking automated. Maintain a strategic distance from crossed arms (guarded), slouched shoulders (powerless) and slumping (worn out or exhausted).

When you create an impression, utilize the correct tone.

The greatest mistake with the manner of speaking, particularly among youthful experts, is speaking up – finishing explanations on an upward affectation so they sound like inquiries. This makes you sound youthful and questionable and here is the way to spot it.

Peruse this sentence so anyone might hear: "I need to go to see that performance." Someone may react: "Me, as well! Would we be able to go at some point this end of the week?"

Presently, read this sentence audibly: "I need to go see that performance?" Did you read "show" and your voice went upward this time? Did it make you wonder in the event that I truly needed to go to the show? That is speaking up. You do not know whether I am expressing something or asking you an inquiry.

On the off chance that you see yourself submitting to this blunder, imagine the sentence you need to state with a period toward the conclusion to complete it unquestionably. In case you are truly not certain you need to create an impression, re-outline your idea into a genuine inquiry.

Make fruitful eye to eye connection.

Eye to eye connection is a basic bit of the nonverbal riddle as it is something that sets up an immediate association among you and your group of spectators. It is particularly basic when you initially welcome somebody, however, it is imperative to look all through a discussion. Studies demonstrate that holding eye to eye connection anyplace between three to five seconds on end is the appropriate way to communicate without transforming the discussion into an intense, frightening gaze.

On the off chance that this is hard for you, attempt these two ideas: either switch forward and backward between looking at one eye and other or look between the eyebrows of the other individual. Both of these alternatives will even now make the eye to eye connection association.

Research has demonstrated that nonverbal segments in communication significantly influence the interpretation of the information we pass on. Since social event components are constantly changing and people are to a great extent uncommon, it is fundamental to lift this consideration regarding nonverbal prompts. Focus on improving your ability to scrutinize nonverbal prompts and you will consider them to be as associations, individual and master, are strengthened.

As you hone your capacities in jumping on nonverbal signs, it is basic to recollect five key measures;

Spot things into the setting. In case someone has their arms crossed it may essentially mean they are nippy. Before coming to a rushed conclusion, put the dialog and the individual into the setting of the subject, timing and other external effects.

Gender, culture, age and geographic territory are essential. A sign may mean by and large various things in different regions. Social and family measures in like manner impact the way we react to nonverbal signs.

Incongruence can mean various things. At whatever point words and nonverbal sign do not alter, our regular detects kick in. Mental bother may exhibit that you are the recipient of distortions, anyway that uneasy tendency may mean various things, as well. Refining one's ability to end up being increasingly open to nonverbal signs can construct one's ability to be more fixed on your own driving forces.

Look out for a mix of signs; It is difficult for our entire bodies to lie. People are fit for disguising their real desires, yet real importance normally spills through various channels.

Trust your intuition. Impulse is the negligent treatment of information (for instance subtle nonverbal sign) appeared as physical assessments. Validity is key since people adequately jump on unauthentic and precarious communication. The more one's thoughtfulness regarding the spoken and the understood, the more one's own driving forces are expanded.

The Seven Principles for Nonverbal Cues

To be an expert in the specialty of nonverbal communications, one must acknowledge where to look and the significance of prompts. There are seven parts of the body that present an entrance to the understood significance of a talk. Improving your general social capacities starts with watching the prompts being sent from each zone only, similarly as all things considered.

The Eyes

The eyes can show perspectives or mental limit. It is noteworthy not to scrutinize a great deal into a nonappearance of eye to eye association since it is essential for certain people to turn away when they are thinking. Eyes can in like manner play out a checking limit. From social to open talking conditions, we can screen our communication suitability by looking and checking their information.

The Face

The face consistently gives the clearest and earth-shattering sign. It is unbelievably expressive, prepared to express unlimited emotions without saying a word. Not in the slightest degree like various zones essentially affected by social measures, outward appearances are the broadest. Specifically, outward appearances for fulfillment, harshness, shock, stun, fear, and sicken are equal across over social orders.

Position

Most events, a person's position passes on their general outlook, conviction and physical success. Take into consideration the manner your perspective on others is influenced by their sitting position, how their heads are held, their walking style and even the way they stand when they enter a room. The way where an individual moves passes on a wealth of information to the world.

The Hands

Hand advancements and sign are the pointers most affected by social or geographic gauges. When working with a worldwide gathering or client, hand movements can have on a very basic level of exceptional criticalness. That being expressed, hands improvements and sign send a colossal proportion of information.

Closeness

Closeness is about a person's position and their space in association with other individuals. Various segments influence how eagerly we sit or stay by someone. The division is regularly managed by social and social benchmarks and the intriguing instances of that partner. The possibility of the subject of trade may in like manner effect expel.

The Feet and Legs

The circumstance of the feet and legs are as often as possible the most genuine markers of authentic significance. The feet and legs fill in as a signal, demonstrating where the individual should need to go if they had the choice.

The feet shows one's status or energy to move. At whatever point, in any event, two people are staying in the talk, watch where the feet are pointing. If the feet are arranged toward within the circle, the individual is secured. Regardless, if one foot is pointing in an outward position—just like one would to expel a phase—that position says, "I am set up to continue forward."

There are various reasons why people do not, for the most part, say what they mean. Understanding the entire importance of any communication infers checking out what is being expressed, yet moreover discovering significance from the understood.

Head Position

The circumstance of your head describes a story and reflects the objective or position. Cutting down the head is a subservient or questionable improvement. This improvement is routinely joined by an inexorably dissuaded or weak position. When the head moves from a downward position to straight or even insignificantly raised, this means that there is startling interest. That improvement snaps the group of spectators afresh into the exchange.

Extraordinary communicators have a wide accumulation of capacities and can modify their communication style in light of the various variables they face at a given time. Here are two or three gauges to consider as you change and refine your social capacities.

Appreciate your gathering of observers; it is basic to understand your group and their trademark tendencies, motivations, goals, troubles, and openings. Does your gathering of onlookers should be heard, lit up, or complete things? What measure of time does your gathering of observers have? Is your group calm and pardoning? It is protected to state that you are associating with a contender, partner, or unparalleled assembling? What desolations and opportunities, real or imaginary, does your gathering of onlookers see? Is there a pariah that is missing whose interest must be directed to empower you to confer even more feasibly? Another bit of understanding your gathering of observers is to be clear about their characteristics and destinations. For example, is your gathering of observers focused on enhancing advantages or social anomalies?

Get yourself; understanding your own personality and what your ordinary tendencies are is the underlying factor to being a convincing and genuine communicator. Are you chatty or do you like to tune in? Is it right to state that you are conclusive? Is it genuine that you are prompt? Is it genuine that you approve of ambiguities, vulnerabilities, and risks? Do you pick your words carefully, or, do you talk continuously like a blundering person?

Do you affront or fail to communicate with others? Do you explode, or do you stay calm and accumulated? Another bit of understanding yourself is to be clear about your characteristics and goals, both when all is said in done and with respect to each communication. When you are certain about for what reason you are bestowing, your valid self will emanate through and add trustworthiness and vitality to your communication. Everything considered, being "certifiable" prompts progressively suitable communication.

Simplify; brief messages that can be passed on quickly and strongly generally have the most amazing impact, especially when you address a gathering of individuals that are depleted or overwhelmed with information. Likewise, these days, who is not depleted or overwhelmed with information? Refining complex materials into absorbable terms that your gathering of onlookers can appreciate and use is a craftsmanship worth looking for after, in light of the way that it regularly has any sort of impact between getting what you need and not. Cut out the particular language and business talk, reduce your multifaceted nature and quit sitting around idly by saying absolutely what you mean in as few words as could be normal in light of the current situation. Moreover consider using delineations, stories, or analogies to adequately express your thought in an even more predominant and significant way.

Find a perfect time; a shrewd idea is simply extraordinary when it comes at the right time. As a convincing communicator, you should be careful with a fortunate opening that empowers you to be the best. For example, offering an answer, thing, or organization precisely when your gathering of onlookers is scanning for one is a perfect time to pass on your message. Believe it or not, keeping an eye on the prerequisites of others in an ideal way is the most guaranteed way to deal with get a perfect outcome and be a ground-breaking communicator. Think about being dynamically alert and versatile in order to even more suitably sway the outcome and get what you need as time goes on.

Listen viably; listening is typically communicational very important part of the communication process. It is not adequate to just tune in, regardless. You need to guarantee that others are heard. In view of that, it is not adequate to just use your ears. Full focus that empowers people to feel heard incorporates eye to eye association, signaling, reasonable and lucky responses, and all around high responsibility. Asking incredible, pertinent requests and a short time later viably listening amasses proclivity and trust. Full focus in like manner incorporates looking for continuously unnoticeable, nonverbal prompts; one's nonverbal communication will as often as possible let you know as much as, if not more than, the substantive message.

Chapter 7 Analyzing Nonverbal Communication

Civilization, in general, can be quite averse to expressions of emotions, especially heightened expressions that tend to disturb the enforced normalcy we're all supposed to maintain. People tend to believe that they shouldn't show other people their feelings because it's the truth about them, so they tend to hide away their emotions. But as we all know, it's almost impossible to hide who you are entirely, and your emotions find some or the other way to be let out.

When we try to suppress our emotions, our brain subconsciously tries to connect with other people so that we can be vulnerable and express what we're feeling. So, even when we consciously might not want someone else to think that we are suffering or have a problem that we're going through, our brain is sending signals through our body language that communicates our need for care and warmth. Body language is essential to human communication, and without it, we probably would need to talk about every little thing that goes through our brain to truly understand each other, which of course, is impossible because even we don't get to access most of our thoughts, needs, and desires. Body language helps us to understand each other without saying things – language can only help us so much in capturing what we think. There are so many feelings and emotions that can't even be described through words, and even when we do describe them, we might not have the right vocabulary to capture what we want to say truly. This gap in communication can only be fulfilled through body language.

Reading body language is ingrained into us because before we developed sophisticated language to communicate with each other, we communicated through body language only. This means that with evolution, we might have forgotten about how to read body language, but our brain hasn't. This is why certain kinds of people attract us more; make us feel more warmth while we instantly have a negative reaction to certain people. Body language triggers in our primal old brains different kinds of emotions, and in turn, can trigger physical reactions in us, like being drawn to a person involuntarily.

Body language is kind of a code that you can just decode by studying different aspects of a person's physique and attitude; if a person is sweating, has clenched fists and a scowl, we can easily decode that this person might be angry and might even be a threat. This is just a simple example; in the modern world, people are quite good at hiding what they're feeling, and an extremely angry man might not even have such simple tells anymore. It might just be simple things like scratching our nose, playing with our hair, etc., that give away our inner feelings. Learning about body language is important not only to understand people better but to make much more sense of our behavior.

How to Analyze

In this part, we're going to take a look at the basics of analyzing people and what are the things that we have to study to determine someone's behavior. Generally speaking, three methods exist to determine someone's behavior – facial profiling, body language, and human psychology.

It's important to remember that some of these methods are far more accurate than other methods. Which method you use also depends a lot on the context you are functioning in and the setting of the place. For example, when you're meeting someone for the first time, you can't read much into their body language because to determine a certain type of behavior, you have to study someone over a period, which is why it's best to stick to facial analysis. Human psychology takes even more time since it requires you to study someone over some time, and you also have to get information from them on their past experiences.

The three different methods in short are:

Facial Profiling

The face can be studied in different contexts to come up with different conclusions. It has been a practice that has been used since ancient Greece to determine people's character and in modern times, has been questioned by many academics. The shape of someone's face does not determine their general demeanor and does not certainly affect who someone is. So, just because someone has a convex shaped face does not mean that they are more likely to be stubborn or aggressive. Your face and its shape have no possible effect on your character as a person.

But, the face does reveal what people are thinking and feeling. By studying someone's face, you might not be able to make a solid conclusion about their character, but you can determine who they are trying to be in that momentary limited context, at least. On the face, you can notice micro-expressions and other similar small details that can reveal someone's intentions and thoughts.

Body Language

Humans wouldn't have been able to form connections and communities if it weren't for body language. For years, we have been able to understand each other and our needs because of body language. Even different cultures have been able to interact with each other only because they were able to use the common language that is stored and represented in our bodies. We can use a simple example to understand how body language works and why it's so effective. If someone is unable to speak for any reason, and if you want to determine if they are okay, they can signal that to you by simply raising their thumb to make the 'okay' sign. The reason why this works is that body language is a common code that is shared by everyone, at least when it comes to using our body to communicate with each other consciously. Culturally, we have all agreed that the 'thumbs up' sign expresses a state of a person signifying that they are all right. It's only when this cultural code is shared by both the person signifying and the person being signified that communication can occur.

When there is a dissonance between our mind and what we want, it's the body that reflects it. This goes to show that it's usually the body that reflects how we feel because we don't have conscious control over it. Since we do have control over what we say, think, and do, they don't necessarily reflect what we want. As an example, think of someone whose feet are almost turned away, most of their body twisted in a way that shows that they wish to leave, but they are still talking to you. By studying their feet, the tension in their body, and the direction their body is trying to face, you can tell if someone is interested in the conversation they're having with you or not. They might still be talking to you because it's the polite thing to do, but it does mean that they're repressing their desire to leave that is manifesting in their body trying to turn them away.

Being able to read body language can help you to be surer of your emotions and other people's emotions. This kind of determinism might be harmful if you apply it to every situation, but when needed, it will give you clarity, instead of leaving you confused about other people's intentions. You can determine if someone is comfortable or not, and change your body language to see it reflect in them responding to this change by becoming more open and comfortable in their body language. Relationships, although considered to be open, can stunt communication with people because of the social pressure of maintaining the illusion of a happy relationship. So, people tend to suppress anything negative, and it might not ever come out verbally, but if you know how to read body language, you can know when your partner is angry or displeased, and you can rectify the situation to ensure that your relationship continues to be as healthy as before.

Human Psychology

Human psychology revolves around understanding human behavior in all its complexity. It's the most difficult method of reading someone but is also the most wholesome in the sense that it covers all reasons for why someone is acting the way that they are. Human psychology doesn't just consider human actions to be a representative of the current environment or state that a person exists in. So, you might think that someone has a certain body language because they are feeling shy, but human psychology will delve into the cause of that shyness manifesting as a fact on this person's body. By studying the past, it might even turn out that this person's shyness was a result of being abused by their parents, who constantly ridiculed them, leading to a reduction in their self-worth, which makes them want to hide away from people.

So, the reading that human psychology elaborates on is one that doesn't consider people as only existing in the present, but recognizes that some people have behavioral issues that have been caused due to their past and their mind might be in the present, but their body still feels the trauma of the past.

Chapter 8 Verbal Communication vs Non-Verbal Communication

In addition to focusing on the words that someone is telling you, it is also important to look at some of the nonverbal cues they are sending out. These are going to include anything that the person does that adds to what they are saying. This could be things like hand movements, eye contact, facial expressions, how they stand, and more. It is pretty much any method that the other person is going to use to communicate, without having to use their words in the process.

If you genuinely want to analyze the other person, you need to have a good idea on how to read other people, and the nonverbal cues they send out. Most people are only able to portray so much when they are talking, but they can tell you so much more when you look at those nonverbal cues. Plus, how many times have you heard someone say something like "I'm fine," and then you see that they can't keep eye contact, or they look sad, and you know the words are false?

While the pertinent key to being successful in all of your relationships are going to rely on your capability of communicating and properly using words, it is not just going to be the words that are utilized that make up all of your communication. Your body language and other nonverbal cues are going to speak so much louder than the words.

When we are talking about nonverbal communication, we are going to look at some options like how much eye contact there is, the tone of voice, the posture of the other person, their hand gestures, and even the expressions that they have on their face. These are all powerful tools of communication that you can use to your advantage if you so wish.

These nonverbal cues can be useful to you as well. If you use them to your advantage, you can put the other person at ease, help to build up some more trust between the two of you, and even draw others into you like there is some connection, even if neither of you knows the other. However, if the nonverbal cues are not sent out the right way, or you choose certain nonverbal cues, it is possible that you are going to send out the wrong message as well.

By being able to improve the way that you use these nonverbal cues, and being able to read them properly, you will find that it is much easier to connect with the others, figure out what they mean no matter what the words say, and can ensure that you build up relationships that are stronger and more rewarding than ever before. And all of this has to come together if you hope ever to analyze the other person.

Why is nonverbal communication important??

Many people wonder why this kind of communication is so important. Why can't we rely on the words that the other person is telling us to ensure that we are set and going to understand what they mean?

Your nonverbal cues, which includes the ways that you react, move, look, and listen are going to tell the other person you are talking to if you do care telling them the truth, and how much you are listening to what they are trying to share with you. When the words that you are telling them seem to match with nonverbal signals that you are sending out, it is going to increase the amount of rapport, clarity, and trust that you get with the other person.

The opposite is going to happen, though when the listener senses that there is not a connection between the words you are using and the nonverbal cues that you are sending out to them. If the listener feels that the two do not match up, it is likely to lead to confusion, mistrust, and tension between the two of you. How likely do you think it is that you will get the other person to listen and even stay in the conversation, so you can analyze them if they don't feel they can trust what you are saying?

This means that if you wish to be better at communicating, and you want to be able to read other people a bit better, then you need not only to become a bit more sensitive to their nonverbal cues and body language but also your own as well.

Now, it is essential to remember here that the nonverbal communication that you are giving out, as well as, the nonverbal communication that you can see from the other person, is going to ply five significant roles. These roles are going to include the following:

1. Repetition: The nonverbal communication can repeat and often strengthen any of the messages that you are trying to make to the other person through your words.

2. Contradictions: If you are not using it properly, the nonverbal cues can contradict the words and the message that is being portrayed through the words. This may tell the listener on the other side that you are confused, or you are lying to them.

3. Substitution: The nonverbal message in some cases can be a substitute of a verbal message. A clear message will be communicated across using facial expressions as compared to use of words.

4. Complementing: Sometimes, the nonverbal cues that you use can complement that verbal message you are sending out. As a manager, for instance, if you do pat the employee on their back along with giving them some praise, it is going to improve the impact that your message is going to have on that person.

5. Accenting: And finally, the nonverbal cues that you are sending out there are going to accentuate or underline the verbal message and can help to get it across. Doing things like pounding the surface of a

table, can help to show the other person the essence of the message you are sending out.

And that brings us to the idea of how you can work to improve your nonverbal communication. If you are already planning out what you want to say in reply to the other person, or you keep checking your phone, or even thinking about a different task that you need to do, then it is 100 percent guaranteed that you are missing out on the nonverbal signs that the other person is sending out to you. And no matter what, missing out on these cues means that you are missing out on some of the subtleties of what is being communicated.

This means that there are ample opportunities for you to go through and improve some of your nonverbal skills. Learning how to be fully present and pay attention to the cues that the other person is sending out to you, and the cues that you are sending out to the other person can help you to learn more about the communication and communicate better with others.

While the words that we say to another person are super important, the nonverbal cues, and the other actions that we go along with the words, can mean just as much, if not more. If you wish to be able to analyze anyone you come across, then it is so vital to be able to understand how the nonverbal communication works. And once you can catch and read these signals, you will be amazed at how much you can learn about the other person, without them even having to say a word.

Chapter 9 Mind Control and How to Influence the Subconscious

First, having gone through in what constitutes body language, the role of body language and how to read body language then it is important that one learns on ways of benefitting from reading the body language of people. In this context, the benefit realized from reading the body language of people is not to torment or use people but rather to enhance your interests that are acceptable such as increasing business deals.

Secondly, mind control refers to a context where one is taken advantage of and appears not to have the mental willpower to understand or control what is happening to him or others. Even though mind control may involve hypnotizing, it mostly occurs without using hypnosis. One of the ways of controlling the mind of another person is to mirror their body language and create a communication rhythm making the person feel connected to you. People that employ mind control are seeking short-term or instant gains, especially by controlling your emotions and how you react to their emotions.

From an ethical viewpoint, mind control largely qualifies as unethical. The moral question arises because one is tapping into the weaknesses of the target person to accomplish your interests. For instance, one can mind control you to make sell an insurance package that you do not need, but the seller needs to be paid. A partner may mind control to enhance loyalty levels in the relationship, which may not be what you are genuinely feeling. As such, with mind control, the question of ethicality dominates the application of mind control.

Fortunately, through understanding body language, one can detect an attempt for controlling their minds and activate defensive measures. First, take note of attempted body language reading to win over a difficult customer or person. At one point, you have encountered a difficult person to understand and get along with despite the best of your efforts. Armed with body language reading competencies, you can correctly analyze their tone, posture, touch, eye contact, and facial expressions to connect with the individual correctly. Similarly, a person trying to control your mind will try to read all these body language cues. For instance, they will employ paralinguistic skills; try to strike a rapport with the person. Some customers are defensive, but if you are armed with, body language reading skills, then you will easily manage to manipulate them to your advantage. Similarly, the manipulating individual will try to apply these tactics on you.

For instance, the manipulating person will try to read if you speak in high-pitched voice, then probably the customer is angry or frustrated by workload or other life issues. Using this knowledge, you can predict how the manipulating person will react to your voice pitch.

Secondly, most manipulators target negative feedback and negative emotions because this is where most people show weakness and create room for mind control. A manipulator will exploit body language to create perceptions of care, love, and sympathy as well as empathy that most people fall for during their challenging moments. By realizing that you are most vulnerable to manipulation when processing negative news and negative emotions, you will be able to manifest high mental awareness levels.

Expectedly, most manipulators that want mind control will seek to precipitate conflict and take advantage of the festering differences. However, by learning and applying effective conflict resolution can be realized by reading the body language of the target person. Assuming that you are an arbiter in a conflict, you should read the body language of the feuding parties to discover any shared ground and the emotive issues. Individuals will show panic, uneasiness, and stiffness when emotive issues are raised such as grinning, crossing arms, breathing fast, and showing cold stare. Individuals will nod if something they agree to is mentioned. They may also stamp their feet, clap hands, and shake hands to show a willingness to talk or strike a compromise.

An arbiter will use reading body language to identify hardliners and use body language to thaw the hard stance of such people. The participants themselves can also read the body language of the other party and appreciate their stance and attempt to initiate meaningful conversation. All these combined efforts will give one an edge in solving conflicts.

Furthermore, watch out for attempts to make conversations interesting. We also would like to enliven conversations, but it is not always the case, and manipulators understand this. One effective way that manipulators use is to improve how other people perceive them is to understand their status and adjust your words and body language. For instance, if a manipulator reads the body language of the other person and realizes that, he or she is feeling disinterested or exhausted; he or she can suggest a break or crack a joke. Through eye contact, you can make the other person feel recognized and wanted to join in the conversation. If the entire group or audience feels disinterested in the conversation by yawning, slouching on their chairs, crossing their legs, and losing eye contact, then the speaker should conduct a quick self-feedback and adjust the communication. It is important to watch out for deliberate attempts to make you attached to the conversation.

Relatedly, taking advantage of reading body language can help one to recognize any dishonesty and pretense in a conversation and help you notice the lack of honesty from the manipulator. Focusing on verbal communication alone is not enough to accurately determine if one is pretending. For instance, your child may say that he is comfortable going out to play while his body language suggests otherwise. For instance, the child could be replying in a high-pitched voice and laugh sarcastically that he or she is comfortable going out to play. The parent will use this body language to address the true feeling of the child. In an intimate relationship, determining the true emotional status of your partner is critical for peaceful and constructive interaction. For instance, if your partner states that she believes you, but her voice is high-pitched, and she is throwing gestures randomly, then chances are that she does not, and, in fact, she is angry with you.

Relatedly exploiting body language reading can make one make a good first impression, and you should critically analyze the first impression. A good first impression is critical when selling, during an interview, and when seeking a life partner. Armed with reading body language one can deliberately enhance positive body language such as nodding to a speech, using gestures when necessary and speaking in a low-pitched voice to sound professional. When one feels tired and wants to shuffle feet or lower eye contact, one can compensate for that by interrupting the speaker to ask a question or take notes. Expectedly, one will offer a firm handshake and accompany it with a smile. Making a good first impression can improve and open opportunities for you in the case of negotiation, interviews, making sales, and seeking a marriage partner.

Furthermore, taking advantage of the body language can help one to correctly identify issues in a relationship by analyzing body language. Apart from just reading the body language and improving social and intimate relationships, one can also use reading body language to determine the presence of issues in relationships, which includes identifying attempts of mind control. For instance, you might notice that when you talk on certain issues with your partner, his or her body language suggests defensiveness and anger. For this reason, reading the body language can help get to the underlying issue even in cases where the partner is determined not to open up. Using body language to identify issues can also help a parent to determine what is bothering a child in cases where the child retreats to its world. The parent can try talking over general issues as well as specific issues and watch the body language of the child to guess the issues or challenges that the child is facing.

Equally important, effectively teaching or sharing ideas can be enhanced by reading the body language of the target audience. A manipulator will seek to adjust the experience to prioritize their needs rather than mutual needs. For instance, a teacher can improve understanding of the students by taking note of signs of lack of concentration such as yawning or staring at the ceiling. However, if the teacher wants to attain mind control, then he or she will manipulate the body language to prioritize only his or her needs over the others. Just like verbal communication, body language can also contain noise where the nonverbal cues of communication distort the intended message. Outside the teaching context, one can improve on sharing ideas by reading the body language of the audience and evoking the desired emotion and reaction. For instance, one should ensure that the target audience is relaxed and alert by evaluating the sitting posture, eye contact, and facial expressions before starting a presentation. Sharing ideas effectively depends on accurate timing and actors, orators, and politicians understand this well.

Finally, taking advantage of reading body language will lead to improved emotional intelligence and social skills to make one more appealing and understanding. Emotional intelligence involves being aware of how you feel and acknowledging how others feel to enhance mutual understanding. For this reason, body language is a critical avenue to read the emotional status of the other person. Emotional intelligence requires correctly reading the emotional status of an individual to enable you to empathize with how they feel. Against this backdrop, reading the body language of a target audience gives an added advantage to an individual to evoke and apply social skills as well as understand self-deeper. Think of speaking to a colleague and manifesting nonverbal cues that you are offended, but the person is not registering what you are feeling. In this context, effective communication will not only be hampered, but the social relationship will also be affected negatively.

Mind Control Techniques

Mind control is recognized as well as exploitation, thinking modification, brainwashing, cerebral power, coercive influence, coercive control, cruel utilization of dynamics of groups, and several other aspects.

The detail that there are such numerous names shows a deficient of conformity which permits perplexity and distortion.

It is acceptable that brainpower comes under the perception of persuasion and power on how to alter people's attitudes and beliefs.

Nevertheless, in addition to this, significant divisions are misplaced in the way.

It's much more practical to perceive influence as a scale.

At one end, there are moral and differential impacts that value the person and his or her privileges.

At the other ending, we have harmful effects that move the person of their individuality, self-sufficiency, and capability to consider in a critical manner or rationally.

So what is brain control?

It is far better to perceive it as a scheme of impacts that considerably interrupts an individual to a large degree, at the altitude of their individuality (their principles, opinions, likings, choices, attitudes, associations, etc.), making a new fake identity or fake personality.

Mind control can be utilized clearly in positive manners, for instance, help addicts, but here we are talking about situations that are innately appalling or immoral.

The social psychologist, Philip Zimbardo, expresses the opinion that brain control is a procedure by which a person or communal liberty of choice and act is compromised by agents or agencies that alter or deform awareness, incentives, influence, cognition, or attitude consequences and he proposes that every person is vulnerable to such treatment.

The person that is mind controlled is not conscious of the influence procedure nor of the alterations happening within themselves.

Persuasion and mind control happen everywhere and are around us all the time. From acquaintances, family units, groups, politicians, religions, scientists, authors, and activists.

The actual query is the following: are we influenced by specifics, cause, investigation, and open admission to data?

Or by controlling and deceptive methods?

I end up to the conclusion that permission through deception is no permission in any way.

Various Mind Control Methods

Fundamental brain control techniques are often shaped widely by cults and sects to employ, instruct, and maintain members, and the greater part of the influential people are psychopaths.

These thoughts about fundamental brain control methods can immediately simply be applied to one-on-one associations as to sets of people.

Narcissists are one more group who frequently use these kinds of methods.

Mind control techniques depending on their utilization can be either seductive or destructive.

They signify diverse things to dissimilar people.

They're also recognized as forced persuasion, brainwashing, thought restructuring, manipulation, and seduction, among others.

Under the umbrella of mind control, there is a sequence of techniques with the intention to manage and alter the mental processes of a human being.

In many cases, they're extremely efficient and, in others, permanent.

In spite of this, not all kinds of cerebral control are essentially negative, because there are some positive uses for these techniques.

Mind control techniques might have very influential effects. They can considerably influence an individual's action, their behaviors, opinions, beliefs, tastes, associations, and even their own identity.

Cerebral control can be used by every person who would like to manipulate or have power over another person.

In addition to that, those people who use these kinds of techniques have very particular reasons, which are either political, social, and/or personal.

Mostly, their aim is for specific people to lose their sense of freedom of thought and personal confidence.

Moreover, mind control is a widespread technique among sects, cults, and religions.

They use them to insert new followers and maintain their members active.

Briefly, mind control isn't always that terrible. These techniques are only negative when they are used for self-serving aims.

In the following page, there are some factual mind control methods that were usually utilized not only by normal individuals in interrelated associations but also in many groups.

Brainwashing

At present, the notion of brainwashing is not used by the majority of psychologists and social scientists, and the techniques of persuasion and compulsion used during the Korean War are not considered to be esoteric.

Hypnotism

Hypnosis is a human situation concerning focused attention, reduced peripheral consciousness, and an improved capability to react to suggestions.

During hypnosis, a person usually has a sharp focus and concentration.

The utilization of hypnosis as a type of therapy to recover and incorporate early trauma is controversial.

Study shows that hypnotizing an individual might, in fact, aid the formation of false-memories.

Hypnotism is an extremely controversial topic, even to the query as to whether it is real or not.

This segment unties a few of these queries and illustrates some of the procedures and methods that are used.

Criticism

Criticism can be utilized as a remoteness aspect.

The manipulators will frequently talk in "us against them" terms, disapprove of the exterior world, and maintain their own superiority.

In accordance with them, you just feel blessed to be around them and be related to them.

Repetition

Steady repetition is an additional authoritative persuasion instrument.

Although it might appear too simple to be effectual, replicating the same message over and over again makes it recognizable and easier to memorize.

When reappearance is shared with communal evidence, it promotes the message without success.

Fear of isolation

New people to controlling groups will typically accept an affectionate welcome and will shape the numeral of new associations that appear to be much deeper and more significant than everything they have ever experienced in their whole life.

As time will pass, if any uncertainties occur, these associations will turn into an influential tool to hold them in the group.

Even if they aren't entirely persuaded, life in the exterior world might appear very lonely for them, and surely they will not want to be isolated and lonely.

Social proof and peer pressure

People who try to control huge groups of people will characteristically use social proof and peer force to brainwash newcomers.

Social evidence is a psychological fact where many people suppose that the movements and attitudes of others are proper and due to the fact that "everyone does that," it must be acceptable.

This turns out to be particularly good when a person isn't sure what to believe, how to act, or what to do.

Numerous individuals in such circumstances will just watch what others do and then do this particular thing.

Fatigue

Exhaustion and sleep deficiency leads to corporal and psychological fatigue.

When you are bodily tired and less alert, you are more vulnerable to influence.

A study referred to in the Journal of Experimental Psychology suggests that people who had not slept for just 21 hours were more vulnerable to persuasion.

Alteration of individuality

Eventually, people manipulate the desire to recreate their individuality.

They desire from you to stop being yourself and turn to a robot, a person who unconsciously goes after their instructions.

Utilizing all techniques and brain manipulation methods mentioned above, they will try to take out an affirmation from you, some form of acknowledgment that you consider that they are good people doing a good thing.

At the start, it may be something apparently unimportant like accepting the fact that the members of the group are fun and loving people or that some of their views are undeniably valid.

When you allow that one little thing, you may be more prepared to admit another one and then another one and then one more. And then before you even know it, out of the desire to be constant with what you do and say, you begin recognizing as one of the group.

This is mainly influential if you are aware that your affirmations were being recorded or filmed.

Chapter 10 Liar! Liar! Pants on Fire! Find Out If A Person Lies or Feels Uncomfortable and How To Exploit It To Their Advantage

How to Determine if Someone Is Lying

Imagine a world where people say the first thing that comes to mind, a world where you told the truth to everyone you talked with.

For example, let's say you took one look at your boss early in the morning only for you to tell him he looks like a weakling.

Or imagine yourself as a salesperson telling a customer how firm and perky her breasts are or a woman telling her male neighbor how nice and tight his butt is.

What do you think would be the result? Peace or chaos? Before I answer that, here's another scenario most people are quite familiar with: your spouse turns around in front of the mirror and asks, "Does this dress make me look fat?" Even if the dress does make her look fat, I know most men will say something along this line, "No, you don't, it's probably the mirror playing tricks on you."

So why do we opt to lie or gloss over some important fact? Well, it is to avoid chaos. As we grow older, we have learned the art of deceit to grease our interactions with others and help us maintain healthy social interactions. We know how much the cold, hard truth hurts sometimes, and it's no wonder research supports the fact that social liars are more popular than those who repeatedly say the truth.

This type of lie is referred to as a white lie since we often know the other person is trying not to hurt our feelings.

Now, what about the malicious lies people tell in order to deliberately deceive others for their personal gain? This is what we are going to focus our attention on. In this chapter, we will take a look at the common cues malicious liars give when they lie or withhold the truth. Before we explore these common deceptions cues, I want you to understand why it's so important to study deception signals.

You and I deserve to know the truth. Society functions on the ability to trust people's words, that people will choose to abide by their words. If it didn't, society would descend into chaos, relationships would have a very short life, there would be no commerce, and parents and children would not trust each other.

In as much as we will sometimes use the white lie to avoid chaos, society also depends on honesty because we would all suffer in the absence of the truth.

Millions of people paid the price with their lives when Adolf Hitler lied to Neville Chamberlain. When Bill Clinton lied, it destroyed the reputation he had built over the years. When

Richard Nixon lied, it nearly broke the steadfast loyalty and confidence of the American citizens to their country. Truth is, undoubtedly, essential in all relations, be it professional or personal.

We are lucky that people speak the truth most of the time and most of the lies we come across are usually social or white lies. When it comes to crucial matters, it is essential for us to assess the truth of what we are told.

It is not always easy finding the truth. For millennia, people had to rely on the use of torture devices to get the truth from those suspected of deception. Today, people have learned how to analyze handwriting and voice and use the polygraph test to know the truth.

Still, even with our advanced techniques, there are a lot of concerns about the accuracy of these methods. You may think you have little chance at succeeding when these modern deception analysis techniques can still fail. Don't be discouraged. With practice, you will become better at reading these deceptions cues.

After all, it is impossible to totally conceal deception.

Why Lying Is Difficult

Practice makes perfect, and most people have spent a good amount of time practicing and honing their lying skills. We have learned how to lie from an early age, and we've done it so often that we have become good at it.

Despite our perceived skills of deception, we still give off nonverbal cues that betray our innermost emotions to the astute observer.

For instance, people tend to smile less when they lie. This is contrary to the popular misconception that we smile more when we lie.

The difficulty in deception is that the subconscious mind gives contrary signals to our verbal statements. That is why it is so easy to catch someone who's not experienced in deception. On the other hand, actors, politicians, and public figures have learned how to refine their body gestures to the level where it's difficult to catch them in a lie. They tend to restrict their gestures in order not to reveal negative or positive gestures when they lie.

Researchers have discovered that it is easier to lie over the phone or an email. It is also easy to lie when part of your body is obscured from the interviewer or interrogator. It is no surprise that law enforcement agencies place their suspect on a chair in the open in a bid to have an unrestricted view of their body language.

How to Detect Deception

People give off different types of signals that reveal deception. Some of these signals are so subtle that even veteran body language readers might miss out on them if they don't know where to look. Some signals are insignificant unless you study them in clusters before you can get an accurate analysis.

In some cases, you will be looking for signals of lies of omission—looking for the hidden piece of information. Other times, you will be searching for signs of lies of commission—verbal statements or actions that are inconsistent with the rest of the message.

Sometimes you won't have access to these deception clues since you might be communicating with the other person via an email or phone call.

Variables such as ethnicity, gender, and cultural background can also influence how you detect nonverbal deception cues. Let's examine the major signs of deception in people.

Study the Body Language

Every part of the human body betrays our true feelings. By studying the arms, legs, eyes, nose, and torso, you can effectively deduce if someone is lying.

Liars Will Try to Avoid Eye Contact

When lying, people often avert their eyes in order not to betray their true emotions. They often do everything in their power to avoid looking at you since they think their lies will be uncovered through their eyes.

Conversely, people often give you their full attention and concentration when they tell the truth.

Restricted Body Movement

The arms and feet are great indicators of negative emotions, like deceit. It is easy to detect the gestures created by these body parts.

When someone is lying, they tend to be less expressive with their arms or hands. This means they are conscious about exposing themselves.

Have you ever noticed your arm movements when you are passionate about something? Your arms will wave all around as you try to emphasize your point.

When you notice a person sitting with his legs and arms close to his body, it's a sign that he's keeping something in. Watch out for unnatural hand and arm gestures. People who lie often try to overcome their restricted body gestures by using their gestures to convince us of the honesty of their verbal statement.

Involuntary Cover-Up

When the person's hand goes straight to the face when making a statement or responding to a question, it is a clear sign of deceit. Liars often cover their mouth while speaking as if they don't believe what they are saying.

Watch Out for Contradictions and Consistencies

In this section, we will take an in-depth look at the correlations between verbal statements and the accompanying body language.

From obvious contradictions, such as shaking your head from side to side while saying yes, to a more subtle form of contradiction, such as a pursed lip, you will learn how to accurately interpret these signals.

You will see that these signs occur both at the conscious and subconscious level. You will notice when people make a conscious effort to embellish their points through their forced gestures and off-timing.

You will also learn how to read people's initial reaction expressions. This is the initial expression you notice on people's faces before they mask it with other body language. Even if you can't read the fleeting initial expression, it is usually an indication that someone had something to hide.

Observe the Timing

Timing is everything when detecting deception. For example, if a person's head begins to shake in an affirmative direction before the words come out, then there's a high chance he's telling the truth. But if the person's head shakes after the point is made, it is a sign that the person is trying to demonstrate conviction.

Watch out for the arm and hand movements that demonstrate a point after it's been made. This gesture is an afterthought, and it's the work of a shoddy liar. These arms and hands movements won't only start late but also seem mechanical and in war with the "verbal" statement. Someone who is truly convicted about his statement will nod or shake the head in tune with every point he makes.

Be aware that a mechanical nodding when there's no point to emphasize is a sign of deception.

Sniff Out the Contradictions

Timing is crucial, but we need to pay more attention to contradictions between verbal and nonverbal cues. The woman who smiles while saying, "I hate you" is sending a contradictory signal. There's an obvious disharmony between her facial expression and verbal statement. Another example is a man telling his girlfriend or spouse he loves while clenching his fists. Similarly, the gesture and the verbal statement are not in harmony.

Study the Timing of the Emotion

It is also difficult to fake the timing of emotions. For you to detect deception, carefully observe the timing of the emotions, and you will never be fooled. A fake emotion is not spontaneous; there's usually a delay in the onset of the emotion. The fake emotion lasts longer than normal and ends abruptly.

Let's take the emotion of surprise to paint this point. The surprise emotion is always fleeting, and it is a fake response if it lasts too long. So when people feign surprise, they usually keep the surprised face longer than usual.

The Unhappy Smile

Here's another contradiction you need to watch out for. I briefly touched this aspect when I explained the concept of smiles. I elaborated on the difference between fake and real smiles and how the former is limited to only the mouth area. When you pay close attention, you will notice that most deception signals are restricted to the mouth region.

Interpersonal Interactions

You need to consider a lot of factors when searching for signs of deception in people. Take a look at their posture in relation to the environment. Observe their stance to see if it's defensive or offensive. Research shows that guilty people are likely to go on the defensive since they feel they feel boxed in. So let's examine the types of cues you will get from someone who's on the defensive.

The Head Shift

When people are not comfortable with their utterance or what they are hearing, they often shift their head away from the one they are talking to. This is an attempt to create a gap from the source of the discomfort. However, you will move your head toward the other person if you are comfortable and secure in your actions.

Take note of the slight conscious withdrawal or pronounced jerking of the head during a conversation. This is an indication of deception or a cover-up. Mind you, never confuse this action with a slight tilt of the head to the side. This gesture occurs when we hear something of interest. It could also function as a vulnerable position.

Check the Posture

Deception breeds insecurity in people, and this is reflected in the body posture. When an individual feels confident or sure about a situation, he sits up straight or stands erect. This also indicates about people feel about themselves.

Liars become unsure of themselves, and it's reflected in their hunched-over body posture. On the other hand, those who are confident about what they are saying will stand straight and walk briskly. You should know that this is not really an effective sign of deception since it is easy to consciously assume this position.

Those Who Walk Away

It is a human instinct to move away from those who pose a problem threat to us. You will never see prey willingly move toward a predator—it is not possible. This instinct is also an important sign for detecting deception. People who feel passionate and confident about what they are saying will often walk toward the other person. On the other hand, people who lie or deceive will angle their body or actually move toward the door.

No Body Contact

When we lie, we often have the feeling that the other person might see through our ruse. Hence, we shy away from any form of physical contact that might betray our real intentions. It is an important sign of deception. The liar will rarely touch the other person during a conversation. Since touch represents a psychological connection, the liar will unconsciously reduce the level of intimacy to hide his guilt.

No Finger Pointing

It's a fact that we all hate having people point their fingers at us. However, it's an indispensable gesture that we are all guilty of when trying to emphasize a point. It emphasizes conviction, and that's what liars generally lack. Therefore, a liar may not be able to use the finger pointing gesture to emphasize a point.

Verbal Content

It is possible to detect deception from verbal statements. The words we use can also provide a glimpse into our inner feelings or emotions. When people wish to deceive, they utilize certain phrase, words, or syntax that they think will portray the truth in their message.

An astute observer will be able to detect words or phrases dressed up as a lie. Here a few clues to detect deception in verbal messages.

When You Get Answers in Your Own Words

Take a moment to notice the way you respond to social greetings when preoccupied. When you walk into a classroom and someone says hi to you, you also respond with hi. At that moment, you are either preoccupied or not interested in making the effort to think.

In this same context, when someone is accused, he will reflect the question of the accuser out of fear of being caught. Why? It's because he's caught off by the question. For example, a furious parent asks, "Did you drink alcohol?" The liars will reply in the negative, "I didn't drink alcohol." You will notice that the word did in the question became didn't?

This is an important clue that the accused is lying since the guilty always wants to get the answers out as fast as possible.

Liars Try More

Someone who is saying the truth will not try to go overboard in convincing you with his answer. A liar will go overboard to ensure that you understand his point in order to prevent further questions on the topic. And he will try to change the topic immediately when he thinks he has convinced you. He will use bold and strong words even if his evidence is fragile.

For instance, if asked if he has cheated in school before, he might answer with "I'm pretty sure I never did." Though, if he is trying to cover up for his past misdeeds, his response is likely to be more elaborate: "No, I would never cheat on a test."

Watch for the Freudian Slip

We are all familiar with the good old slip of the tongue. We sometimes say one thing when we mean to say another. Most times, these slip of the tongue or subconscious leaks reflect our inner emotions or feelings.

For example, a baker who might mean to say, "I baked the cake all by myself all through the night," might slip and say, "We baked the cake together by working all through the night." Although Freudian slips are great indicators of a person's inner thoughts, their occurrence is unpredictable.

Beware of Those Who Depersonalize Questions

Watch out for those who depersonalize your question since there's a high chance they are lying to you.

Let's say you asked a former employee, "Did you steal from your previous boss?" Watch if you get a reply along the lines of "No, I think stealing is the worst thing any human could ever do."

As you can see from the example, the liar has successfully thwarted the answer in an impersonal way. The liar might also go further by saying, "You know I abhor such things. I think it is morally repulsive."

Liars Get Uncomfortable with Silence

Silence holds a lot of meaning, and for the liar, it means the other person is not buying what they are saying. They become more uncomfortable as the silence stretches far longer than necessary.

When you ask someone a question, observe if he supplies more answers without being prodded.

Here's a typical scenario you often see in movies: Mr. Peter is sitting before a police officer in an interrogation room. The investigator asks Peter about his whereabouts on the night of a crime scene, and he responds with "I was having a blast with my friends at the club downtown." However, the investigator doesn't acknowledge his answer. Rather, he stays silent and stares at Peter. As the silence becomes unbearable, Peter becomes nervous and goes on to add more unsolicited facts that actually implicates him in the end.

The guilty will always get spooked by the silence and will tell his story in pieces until he gets a verbal confirmation to stop taking.

The Implied Answer Is No Answer

Here's a sign of deception you need to watch out for. Watch out for those who skirt around answering your question and instead give you an implied answer.

For instance, you are talking to a girl over the phone, and you asked her if she was gorgeous. If she proceeds to tell you that she works out three times a day, eats healthy, and jogs around the block in the evening, then she has given you an implied answer.

She is trying to circumvent the question by implying that she is gorgeous.

How the Words Are Conveyed

Here's a question for you: why do you think some company salespeople sell more than others in that same company despite reading the same sales material and selling the same product?

What makes the difference? I believe the answer lies in the difference in the way they convey their words. How something is said is just as important as what is said. So let's examine how you can use word delivery to detect deception.

Study the Speed of Answers

A restaurant uses the speedy answer test to employ workers. Here's how it works. They will ask the employee if he has any prejudice against those from different racial groups or different sexual preferences. The longer it takes for the interviewee to answer, the lower the score.

Since the question has to do with beliefs, it takes a longer time for the mind to process. Therefore, someone who holds no prejudice or discrimination answers quickly. A prejudiced person will take time to come up with the "right" or dishonest answer—no one wants to be seen as prejudiced.

If, however, a prejudiced person is able to come up with a fast answer, the interviewer then observes how fast the rest of the sentences follow the initial yes or no response. Those speaking the truth will immediately follow their initial one-word response with an explanation. If the person is deceitful, the rest of the sentence will come slowly after the initial response.

Liars Often Shy Away from Laying Emphasis

A liar will often try to limit his ownership and commitment to his replies. Pronouns such as us, we, and I are underutilized in his replies. When someone speaks the truth, he will often make use of the possessive pronouns as much as the rest of his statement.

For instance, a truthful person will reply in the affirmatively by saying, "Yes, I am." A liar may respond with a simple yes.

A liar may not place emphasis on words of expression, and he will often try to reduce ownership of his words.

For instance, a liar will quickly say, "It went great," instead of saying, "We had a greeeat time!" which is more expressive and committed than the former.

The Mumbler

Have you ever noticed that kids tend to mumble their answers when lying? They will often look down and place their hands behind their backs while mumbling a lie.

Note that this response is not limited to lying; it could also reveal shyness. The mumbling gesture is also effective in detecting deception. A liar is likely to mumble his answers since he is unsure of his answers.

Someone who's passionate about what he's saying will increase the volume of his voice and speak faster.

Analyzing Questions and Statements

If you are a keen observer, you will notice that questions and statements have different speaking styles. Let me explain.

When you ask someone, "What are you doing?" you will notice that the head comes up at the -ing part of the question. The eyes also widen at that last part of the question.

If the person replies with a statement that is styled like a question, then he is unsure of his statement and searching for verbal confirmation from you. However, if he replies with certainty, then he is confident and truthful about his reply.

Psychological Profile

These signs of deceit show how liars think and what characteristics are missing from a story that makes it fictitious.

It Takes a Thief to Know a Thief

The way we see the world is a reflection of how we see ourselves. Someone who sees the world as a cesspool of corruption, lies, and greed may be full of these negatives.

Watch out for those who are quick to point out faults in others as they are likely to have those qualities themselves. That is why a con artist is always the first to accuse another of cheating.

If someone out of the blue accuses you of cheating or lying, ask yourself, "Why is this person so paranoid?" It is possible that this person is projecting their own qualities on you. So watch for these clues since they are often signs of deception.

Another Dimension in the Story

Liars aren't always great storytellers; they often omit the crucial element when telling a story—another person's point of view. This is because most liars are not clever enough to add a third dimension to the story to give it more flesh. While the liar includes the other person in his story, he may omit the person's thoughts in the story.

This is not a clear sign of deception, but it is more believable if you include other people's thoughts in your story.

Let's say you asked your spouse about her whereabouts the previous night. In response to your question, she told you that she worked late. However, you are not convinced and decide to press further and asked what she had for dinner that night. Here are two answers she might give you:

"I didn't really feel hungry last night. So I came home and played a game with my roommate. She made a casserole, but I passed on it."

"I didn't really feel hungry last night. So I came home and played a game with my roommate. My roommate was aghast that I would actually skip dinner, especially her signature casserole dish."

Tell me, which version is more convincing, the former or the latter. Although both versions contain the same information, the latter adds another layer of thought—the opinion of a second party.

Fewer Negatives in a Story

When someone tells you a made-up story, you will often notice the absence of negatives in the story. A liar will only focus on getting the story right. Therefore, he will stick to primary thoughts which are positives since negative is not a primary thought.

For instance, ask a friend about his vacation. He will cover both the positive and negative aspects of the journey, such as sunny and clear weather or the mix-up in travel bags.

Conversely, when someone makes up a story about their vacation, you will notice the absence of negatives in the story. There is a clause to this clue: "If the person is explaining about why he was delayed, then you should expect to hear some negatives."

Rarely Believe Anyone Who Says This

There's no more obvious cue to detect liars than those who start their statements with phrases such as "To be frank," "To tell you the truth," "To be perfectly honest." Be cautious about believing those who use these phrases as the next thing that comes after these phrases is often a lie.

Someone who tells the truth doesn't need to use these phrases to convince you—although some people have made a habit of using these phrases all the time, and it might not be an indication of deceit.

For those who don't use these expressions habitually, then it's a likely sign of deceit. So watch out if these phrases are not part of a person's verbal repertoire.

Also watch out for persuasive phrases like "Why would I lie to you?" and "You know I would never lie to you.

Chapter 11 How To Falsify Body Language To Exploit It In Your Favor

The next thing that we need to take a look at is how to fake your body language. Some people feel that faking this kind of thing is impossible. They know that it is hard to hide a lot of the body signs that you are trying to show to others. This doesn't mean that the process is impossible to work with, but it does take a lot of time and effort to do.

Faking body language is not easy because there is always something that is going to sell you out. It could be the eyes are not accompanying the smile, the hands are not accompanying the words, and the head is not following the hands and many more others. However, despite the entire sell out, body language faking can be learned so it means it is possible to fake your body language. You do not need to fake 100 percent of your body language because there will be a hitch, but you can always fake 70 percent of it. For you to fake your body language, you must first understand how to learn and interpret the body language. It is like a basketball game, you cannot be good at basketball if you haven't learned about its rule, the risks involved, the importance of the game and the remedy if you are not achieving the expected results.

Many people are not aware of the different body languages and nonverbal language cues that they send out to the world. But this doesn't mean that you are not able to fake some of it, and get others to think that you feel and act in a certain way. Keep in mind here that doing this is going to be difficult sometimes. It is not always as easy as it seems, and you have to be constantly aware of what you are doing. If you forget to do this and aren't paying attention to the different parts of your body language and how they are working together, you will find that some part of you will betray you, and you lose the trust in the person you are trying to work with.

The good news here is that with a little bit of practice and some hard thinking at the same time, you can control the various aspects of your personality and figure out how to make people see different things with your body language. There are different ways you can fake your body language to suit your desires. Some of the things that you should focus on include:

Taking In A Deep Breath

When talking to someone whether you are giving a speech to the audience or you are listening to them, you should watch both the breathing rate and the other persons. The breathing rate of a person tells much about your emotions. Breathing of a person and his emotions are highly connected so you must be very careful with your rate of breathing if you want to fake it. When someone breaths deeply, it might show that he is afraid. A person holding his breath for some time than breathing deeply shows that the person is afraid. For example, a child who knows that after telling his mother that he licked sugar will be beaten, no matter how the mother asks him; he will simply breathe deeply without speaking.

He is sending a message to his mother that he is afraid that if he speaks, he will be beaten. So if you are afraid and you do not want to show the other person, you want to feel more superior, you want to prove that you are not afraid of doing anything or you are not afraid of the other person, make sure your breathing rate is balanced. You should not breathe in deeply once after he has asked a question, take time breathing normally, you can hold your breath a little bit then start breathing normally, someone won't recognize the fear you are experiencing.

Taking a deep breath may also signify anger. When someone is angry, he has no control over the thing or the one upsetting him. Just like fear, anger is emotional and like we said emotional feelings are connected to breathing. When you are so upset and so angry, watch your breathing rate if you do not want to show it. To fake your breathing rate, you can smile a bit and sip some water if there is any in the glass instead of breathing deeply. Maintain your eye contact and think of funny things in your past, use humor, like crack a funny joke when the person aiming to make you angry says an awful thing, you can also repeat a calming phrase within your head like 'take is fine, take it easy'. This will help calm you down and you will realize your breathing rate is normal.

Deep breath also shows excitement. This could be excitement from receiving after party. You sit down to think about it, you hold your breath while thinking about it then you breathe in so deeply. You are excited that it was a wonderful party, but if you happened to sneak out of the house and go for this wonderful party and you come back to find your parents waiting for you, you have to fake it because party on a school day is guaranteed with punishment. To fake it you should make sure you do not breathe deep in with a wide smile on your face. Not doing this will make your parents see your excitement and know what you were up to.

When someone is relieved, he is likely to take a deep breath. Thus taking a deep breath signifies relief. You may have been fighting with someone over a piece of land for a year, and then he comes to you and says he has let it go, you can have it. This is a relief. You will take a deep breath for that. You can always fake this so that he can see how tiring the case was to you.

When you breathe in deeply, it might also show shock, surprise which is always accompanied by a head sign, love attraction, hopelessness or sadness. If you have to fake all these, you must make sure your breathing stays normal no matter how much these feelings flood your mind. To make sure you want to fake all your emotional traumas or feelings without anyone knowing they are fake; it is also good that you identify your emotional triggers. This will help you be in charge of your emotions and each time any trigger is pressed, you will find yourself smiling about it and it will not affect you. This way you would have faked it beyond any doubt.

The Eye Contact

The first thing that we are going to focus on when we need to fake our body language is going to be eye contact. You need to make sure that your eye contact is on point. This is one of the easiest things to fake, and if you are messing up with this still in your personal and professional life, then it means that you are going to have to work on that before you get a chance to work with some of the others.

Think about the last time you talked with someone who was not able to maintain eye contact. Whether it was them focusing down all of the time, them looking at their phone or their watch, or even glancing towards the door all of the time, it felt like they wanted to look anywhere but at you. Eventually, it made you feel like you were not important, and you wanted to stop the conversation and move on, no matter how important the information was.

Don't be like this person. You don't want to make the other person feel like they are not important. You want them to know that you are interested in them, that what they have to say is worth your attention. And the best way to do this is to make sure that your eye contact is good.

There is a nice balance here. You do not want your gaze to be so intense that you make the other person feel uncomfortable. We all know this kind of gaze. It includes no blinking and may feel like you are trying to do a stare down with the other person.

Focus on a gaze that shows that you are interested, but include some blinking and some emotion in them as well.

Controlling the movement of your eyebrows

The eyebrow movement will tell what you are thinking and the message you are trying to pass across. By lowering your eyebrows when speaking to someone it will send a variety of messages. When your eyebrows are lowered, it shows deception. You will be concealing something from the audience or the speaker. If you want to fake this even if you are hiding something, make sure your eyebrows are raised humbly. This will send a different message. Lowered eyebrows also show desire. The desire that the eyes cannot see or are afraid to view. For example in a love relationship, when a partner asks for a kiss, you might find yourself lowering your eyebrows. This is sending a message that you have the desire to kiss but you can't say it, or the eyes can't help it. If you want to fake this so that the other person does not see that you have no desire, you can act surprised by raising your eyebrows with your eyes open wide or do exactly what is required. This will tell the person of your surprise or your desires in the kiss too.

A person lowering eyebrows may also be annoyed. Annoyance may be caused by a variety of things and he is afraid that if he raises his eyes he might cry or be tempted to say something bad. If you want to fake it so that nobody can know if you are annoyed, you can start breathing in and then out as you count, or focus on the main aim of the conversation and you will realize that your annoyance is subsiding and while doing all this, let ensure your eyebrows haven't changed their former position.

Raised eyebrows may signify attention request or demand depending on the question posed before the raising.

Demanding for attention with raised eyebrows is seen rude sometimes especially if it is coming from a child to a parent or a younger person to an older on so you should be careful if you have this habit. Faking this raising of eyebrows when asking for attention, you may show attraction instead, when someone sees attraction in the eyes, he will give the attention you want. This attraction can be done by raising your eyebrows to expose your eyes.

Submission can also be symbolized by raised eyebrows. For example, a person asking you if you are going to lend him money, and you raise tour eyebrows. This means you have submitted to his request and he will get the money. But if you do not want the person to see that you are forcing this submission, you can as well lower your eyebrows, he will be confused and won't tell if it is a yes or no or you can raise your eyebrows with the eyes looking up, this will tell the person that you are thinking about it.

Raising one eyebrow can also indicate cynicism especially when the other person is speaking inaccurately. The other person may feel offended if he saw you cynically raising your eyebrows thus to fake it, you can stay with your eyebrows normal but focus your mind on something else. When he is done talking you greet each other and leave like nothing ever happened. Most of the psychologists use this faking especially to the clients who are so depressed and are speaking things that do not make sense, the psychologists even go ahead and nod their heads while the clients are speaking then they can now paraphrase their words to get clarification otherwise raising one eyebrow to them will confuse them more and they will be annoyed that they are not getting the help they needed.

Pushing together your eyebrows and pulling up your forehead indicated relief. For example, you have been waiting for a whole day for some news from the interview you attended, then finally the results come and you have passed. This is a great relief and you will feel your nerves calming down. This way your eyebrows will be pushed together, and forehead pulled up. To make sure that someone believes in this you as it is written. Anxiety can also be seen when the eyebrows are pushed together, and the forehead pulled up. You can fake anxiety especially when you want to get out of a boring meeting that you have by saying you have to see a doctor. The show of anxiety on your face can get you permission to step out.

Relaxing your face

A relaxed face is not a compressed face. A relaxed face can easily be seen by the facial muscles. The muscles are flexed, the eyebrows not clenched together, the forehead is not wrinkled or creased, the eyes are not tensed and the lips are full. All these describe a relaxed face. If anything from the above is opposite, this means you do not have a relaxed face and anyone can be able to tell what is bothering you. To fake a relaxed face, you have to understand the following facial meanings;

A relaxed face shows control of emotions. It tells that you are in control of what is going on around you.

For example, you indulge in an argument at the office with your co-worker, the shouting is so high from your fellow worker that the other workers come in, just by the calmness on your face, and the other workers will see control of your emotions. They will know that you have the situation under control and it is not bothering you.

If you are a businessperson and you want to show people that they can count on you, you must have a relaxed face. Relaxed faces show responsibility. Especially when there is a problem in the office and people are confused, by maintaining a relaxed face, people tend to see you as more responsible and they will be counting on you to provide the solutions to any problems arising. Most magnetic leaders are experts at this. They always maintain calm faces even when the going is so rough because they know people are counting on them.

When you are in control of things happening around you it is seen from your calm face. For example, you receive a call from the office that the workers are rioting, the police have been called to disburse then, but the situation is still rampant. S you decide to go to the office, with a calm face you call upon the workers, and they all stop whatever they are doing and start listening to you address their concerns. The calmness on your face will tell anyone that comes to that meeting that you have got control over your face even when deep within you know you are not calm.

If you want people to respect you, make sure your face is calm especially during stress. When you are so hurt and stressed up, people will always see it on your face. But when your face seems so calm with no sign of stress, this will pull them towards you, they will respect you and most of them will want to emulate you. They will see a person that is a good example who is in control and can lead. A calm face will also make someone see honesty in you. When you are speaking to someone after a mistake has been committed, your face will let the person know if you are honest or not. For example in school, when something wrong has happened and the teacher calls you to the staffroom, the calmness of your face will teacher that you are honest in whatever you are saying. So faking a calm face will make you get anything you want to.

Your Arm Movements

Pay attention to the arm movements that you are doing. If you want to be able to show another person that you are excited and happy about something, it probably is not a good idea to stand with the arms crossed. Happiness and excitement are going to include a lot of arm movements going all of the time. The bigger the movements (within reason, don't try to hit the other person with the flailing arms), the more animated you are going to appear to others as well.

However, if you want to appear like you are calm and collected, or like you are more withdrawn (there may be times when you want someone to leave you alone for example), then crossing your arms, or at least keeping the arms and hands close to the body, may be the right option for your needs.

So, when you are trying to fake your arm movements as a part of the body language, the best way to do this is to figure out what mood you want to portray to the other person. If you want to show that you are animated and excited, then the arm movements need to be away from the body and nice and big. If you're going to show that you are more withdrawn, then the arms and hands need to be close to the body.

The Smile

It is important to spend some time focusing on the smile that you give off. Many of us have been trained on how to give a fake smile in any situation, but there is a big difference between the fake smile and a genuine smile. You may be able to fake it with some people, but often, you need to try and get a real and genuine smile on your face to impress those around you.

Remember that with a genuine smile, you need to use more than the sides of the mouth. This one includes the whole face and even some crinkles around the eyes. This can be done even when faking it, but you need to do some practice. An excellent way to do this is to spend some time in a mirror, working on the smile, and trying to get the whole face into it.

Doing a smile in front of the mirror is going to make a big difference. You can look at how the smile will appear to others, and get a general feel of how it is going to feel to do this. Then, when you are in front of someone else using this smile, without the mirror present, you will know how to make this smile appear for you.

Speaking In Balanced Tones

Tones involve the volume you use and the emphasis you place on every word. When the emphasis is placed on different words, the meanings of words change. When different tones are applied to different words, it changes the emotional influence on the words. For example, someone saying politely while joking 'you are stupid' it will sound funny and a joke and emotionally it won't hurt you unlike someone speaking in a firm tone with serious telling you the same. The emotional attachment to the first incidence and the second incidence differs because of tonal variation.

Supporting Your Head

How you support your head while talking tells more than you think. When your head is supported at the chin position horizontally with the chin lifted, this is a show of superiority. Most managers like sitting in this position in the meetings while listening to the views of the junior staff. This is an expression that they are superior over the others. Faking this is easy as long as you do not lose your focus. When you clasp your hands at the back of your head with the elbows spread out, this indicates that you are confident enough. You are confident about what you are talking about and at the same time, it signifies superiority and dominance. For example, a person is trying to send the message that 'I know this very wee and I am the boss'. This happens mostly after someone has finished a certain project.

Sometimes clasping the hands at the back of your head while facing the opposite side of a person who is demanding something from you may show submission. This is mostly seen when the police are making arrests. The police tell you to put your hands at the back of your head so that they can search for you. When you comply, it shows you have submitted to the command or request of the being issued.

When you support your head sideways it sends different messages. You could be tired and you just need some relaxing especially when you support your head with your eyes closed. It could also mean that you are indeed thought when you support your head with your hands on your forehead looking down. Supporting your head sideways with focus on the speaker and a smile can also indicate admiration. This happens mostly when people are on a love date.

Supporting your head by putting the hands on your head may show regret. This mostly is seen when football players have missed a penalty or a goal chance.

Your Stance

The last thing that we are going to look at is your stance. You need to make sure that you are picking out the right kind of stance to impress another person and let them know that you are interested. Of course, the posture is going to be an important part of all of this. You want to stand upright, rather than to slouch, and you want to make sure that you show off the confidence that is inside of you.

There is more to this one than just the posture that you use, though. If you can add a few more things into this, you will find out that it is going to help you to get some results with how comfortable others are around you. The first thing to look at is your feet. If you want the other person to think that you are interested in them and that your whole attention is on them, then make sure the feet are pointed in the right direction. They need to be pointed at the person you are talking to, rather than to the side or even worse, towards the door.

The way that you lean is important as well. If your posture has you leaning towards the door, or at all away from the other person, then this is going to give them the thought that you are not interested in them at all. But, if you are leaning slightly towards them, with your body leaning in, it shows that you are interested in what they are saying to them.

It is hard to fake the body language that you are doing with another person. While we often wish to show off a certain kind of appearance to others, it is going to be tough to do this. You have to be careful about how you do this. But with some practice and tips shared here, you will become more aware of the different cues that our bodies are giving off to others, and it is a lot easier for you to give off the appearance that you would like.

Chapter 12 What Is Dark Psychology and How to Use it

Dark Psychology is a branch of psychology that fascinates people across the globe who are interested in topics like understanding the criminal mind, better understanding the darker thoughts that control human behavior at all ages, and the conscious actions people take to influence others using psychological manipulation.

At its core, Dark Psychology is the specified study of the more wicked side to human nature: what defines it, how to observe it, where the lines are and how it can be used for both beneficial and nefarious purposes. It covers mild uses like a clever car salesman who continuously has the best sales numbers on his team because he is able to read his customers and build an amiable connection with them based on observations to the severe uses like studying the mind of criminals who use their understanding of human behavior to victimize others.

The bleak title may make some hesitate before trying to understand the subject, but the truth is that many of the elements of Dark Psychology are in use (sometimes intentionally, sometimes unconsciously) in everyone's daily interactions and communications with other people from friends and family to clients or even perfect strangers.

Dark Psychology can be used for a variety of reasons that benefits the individual practicing the methods and techniques while helping the master a greater understanding of the darker sides of human nature, communication and relationships. One of the main uses for Dark Psychology and its particular methods is the manipulation of others' thoughts, feelings and actions through emotional control and persuasion.

People with the types of personalities that don't hesitate to benefit from using Dark Psychology to manipulate others and boost their own advancement have been shown to gravitate toward certain career paths. These techniques are often used by people in the following industries to advance their careers:

- CEOs and company presidents

- Criminal investigators and the criminals they profile

- Prison psychologists and those who work to help people identify and understand their darker instincts, inclinations or impulses

- Artists, actors, writers and others who focus on artistic pursuits in the interest of gaining the admiration of others

Career personality studies have also shown that those people who rely on Dark Psychology to further their careers or their position in life may not necessarily have darker personality traits, especially since these are skills and methods that can be learned and practiced by just about anyone. However, people can also just develop some of the darker manipulation techniques from having a shadier side to their personality. Those who have not taken the extra step to collect these skills are the most adept at using them and hiding their use of them as they've had since childhood to start practice and perfect them.

Depending on the goals of the person practicing the Dark Psychology techniques, they can be put to use for almost any purpose when trying to understand the true nature of a person.

Conclusion

Now you know how to read people like a book. Your life will become so much easier now that you have finished this book and learned the critical life skill of reading other people.

You can become a better person by knowing how to read people. Reading people allows you to develop empathy. You can tell what others are feeling and respond accordingly. Your sensitivity will make you a more responsive and caring lover, parent, friend, and family member.

You can also protect yourself better from the harm of people with bad intentions. When you are able to read people, you are consequently able to spot people that will not benefit you. Before you get too far into a relationship of any nature with someone harmful, you can see what the person is about and prevent further harm from happening.

Here are a few points to summarize:

It is not very realistic to expect that most of us will develop the kind of extra-sensory perception that will make us mind readers. However, all people can learn to identify the non-verbal clues that others demonstrate every day. These psychological tips will make you understand people perfectly in no time.

Most of the time we do not stop to think about the language of our body, what we transmit in non-verbal communication. It is even more important than the words we use, gestures, posture and facial expression reveal more than we can suppose or intend to demonstrate. To have control of these movements is to be able to pass the message of the emotions and thoughts in a balanced way, reinforcing the words with the gestures. Research indicates that only 7% of our communication is word-based. The body language is responsible for another 55% and the tone of voice for 38%.

A negative body language can convey weakness, insecurity. And we do not want our interlocutor to have that impression. Having the knowledge and mastery of our body makes a lot of difference in personal and professional relationships from the moment we recognize their power. A correct and upright posture requires training and corrections until you reach perfection. Sitting in the right way according to the environment, without exposing yourself too much, demonstrates education. Standing without arms crossed or hands in pockets conveys confidence and security. Walking elegantly, even with very high heels, without much movement in the hips and without looking at the ground, projects positivity. The body should always be moved smoothly, without sudden movements or drama.

Accelerated or aggressive rhythm generates a sense of stress and lack of confidence. Carrying your hand over your mouth while talking or looking away from the caller gives the impression of lying. The look, then, is extremely revealing. No matter how hard we try to hide our emotions, it shows the truth of our feelings.

How many times do we say one thing believing another? Those who pay attention to their eyes will realize how much truthfulness there is in words. An unfocused look can be confusing as if you are looking for a mental image for support. The famous twist of eyes denotes irritation and contempt. To contact the forehead means tension, doubt or nervousness, a very negative point. Crossing one's arms away from the others, representing the imposition of a physical barrier, that is, no opening as to what is being said. On the plus side, a firm handshake demonstrates confidence. Speaking calmly, articulating the words well and maintaining tranquility, conveys credibility. Who believes in someone who does not express himself correctly, speaks in a fiddly way, without coherence of thoughts?

Knowledge and mastery of body language techniques add value to our relationships in any environment. Analyzing and learning how to deal with our gestural is a differential in social relations, there is no denying.

Let me paint a bigger picture here the world is made of over 6 billion people and while you may not get to connect with every one of those people throughout your lifetime, it is important that the relationships that you have in your world are built on solid foundations that are beneficial to everyone involved. And this process starts with you. Thankfully, you have read this book and gotten a head start how to make that process happen. People will learn from you and replicate the efforts you have put into the relationships and their other relationships as well. Think of it as a ripple effect; and the chain reaction that this would build over time.

When it comes to choosing a good friend or lover, you are now better able to pick people that are good for your life. You can spot those that actually care for you and have the capability of treating you well. You can pick lovers and friends that have good track records.

All of these benefits are now yours. Thanks for reading.

www.ingramcontent.com/pod-product-compliance
Lightning Source LLC
Chambersburg PA
CBHW070714250726
48662CB00001B/403